YEAR B
AFTER PENTECOST 1

YEAR **B**
AFTER PENTECOST **1**

PREACHING
THE REVISED
COMMON
LECTIONARY

Marion Soards
Thomas Dozeman
Kendall McCabe

ABINGDON PRESS
Nashville

PREACHING THE REVISED COMMON LECTIONARY
YEAR B: AFTER PENTECOST 1

Copyright © 1993 by Abingdon Press

This book is printed on recycled, acid-free paper.

Library of Congress Cataloging-in-Publication Data
(Revised for vol. 3)
Soards, Marion L., 1952–
Preaching the revised common lectionary.

Contents: [1] Advent/Christmas Epiphany—
[3] After Pentecost 1
1. Bible—Homiletical use. 2. Lectionary preaching.
I. Dozeman, Thomas B. II. McCabe, Kendall, 1939–
III. Common lectionary (1992). IV. Title.
BS534.5.S63 1993   251   92-36840
ISBN 0-687-33802-6 (v. 1: alk. paper)
ISBN 0-687-33803-4 (v. 2 : alk. paper)
ISBN 0-687-33877-8 (v. 3: alk. paper)

You may order the software edition of *Preaching the Revised Common Lectionary,* packaged in Year A, B, or C from your local religious bookstore, or by calling 1-800-672-1789. Specify whether your computer system is running at least DOS 3.0 or Windows.

Scripture quotations, unless otherwise noted, are from the New Revised Standard Version of the Bible, copyright © 1989 by the Division of Christian Education of the National Council of the Churches of Christ in the USA. Used by permission.

97 98 99 00 01 02 — 10 9 8 7 6 5 4 3

MANUFACTURED IN THE UNITED STATES OF AMERICA

Contents

CONTENTS

Introduction

Now pastors and students have a systematic treatment of essential issues of the Christian year and Bible study for worship and proclamation based on the Revised Common Lectionary. Interpretation of the lectionary will separate into three parts: Calendar, Canon, and Celebration. A brief word of introduction will provide helpful guidelines for utilizing this resource in worship through the Christian year.

Calendar. Every season of the Christian year will be introduced with a theological interpretation of its meaning, and how it relates to the overall Christian year. This section will also include specific liturgical suggestions for the season.

Canon. The lectionary passages will be interpreted in terms of their setting, structure, and significance. First, the word *setting* is being used loosely in this commentary to include a range of different contexts in which biblical texts can be interpreted from literary setting to historical or cultic settings. Second, regardless of how the text is approached under the heading of setting, interpretation will always proceed to an analysis of the structure of the text under study. Third, under the heading of significance, central themes and motifs of the passage will be underscored to provide a theological interpretation of the text as a springboard for preaching. Thus interpretation of the lectionary passages will result in the outline on the next page.

Celebration. This section will focus on specific ways of relating the lessons to liturgical acts and/or homiletical options for the day on which they occur. How the texts have been used in the Christian tradition will sometimes be illustrated to stimulate the thinking of preachers and planners of worship services.

I. OLD TESTAMENT TEXTS

A. The Old Testament Lesson

1. *Setting*
2. *Structure*
3. *Significance*

B. Psalm

1. *Setting*
2. *Structure*
3. *Significance*

II. NEW TESTAMENT TEXTS

A. The Epistle

1. *Setting*
2. *Structure*
3. *Significance*

B. The Gospel

1. *Setting*
2. *Structure*
3. *Significance*

Why We Use the Lectionary

Although many denominations have been officially or unofficially using some form of the lectionary for many years some pastors are still unclear about where it comes from, why some lectionaries differ from denomination to denomination, and why the use of a lectionary is to be preferred to a more random sampling of scripture.

Simply put, the use of a lectionary guarantees a more diverse scriptural diet for God's people, and it can help protect the congregation from the whims and prejudices of the pastor and other worship planners. Faithful use of the lectionary means that preachers must deal with texts they had rather ignore, but about which the congregation may have great concern and interest. Jesus' insistence in John 6 on the necessity of eating his flesh and drinking his blood, which we encounter in this volume, might be a case in point. Adherence to the lectionary can be an antidote to that homiletical arrogance that says, "I know what my people need," and in humility acknowledges that the Word of God found in scripture may speak to more needs on Sunday morning than we even know exist, when we seek to proclaim faithfully the message we have wrestled from the text.

The lectionary may also serve as a resource for liturgical content. The psalm is intended to be a response to the Old Testament lesson, and not read as a lesson itself, but beyond that the lessons may inform the content of prayers of confession, intercession, and petition. Some lessons may be adapted as affirmations of faith, as in *The United Methodist Hymnal*, nos. 887-89; the United Church of Christ's *Hymnal*, nos. 429-30; and the Presbyterian *Worshipbook*, no. 30. The "Celebration" entries for each day will call attention to these opportunities from time to time.

Pastors and preachers in the free-church tradition should think of the lectionary as a primary resource for preaching and worship, but need to remember that the lectionary was made for them and not they for the lectionary. The lectionary may serve as the inspiration for a separate series of lessons and sermons that will include texts not in the present edition, or having chosen one of the lectionary passages as the basis for the day's sermon, the preacher may wish to make an independent choice of the other lessons in order to supplement and illustrate the primary text. The lectionary will be of most value when its use is not a cause for legalism but for inspiration.

Just as there are no perfect preachers, so there are no perfect lectionaries. The Revised Common Lectionary, upon which this series is based, is the result of the work of many years by the Consultation on Common Texts and is a response to ongoing evaluation of the *Common Lectionary* (1983) by pastors and scholars from the several participating denominations. The current interest in the lectionary can be traced back to the Second Vatican Council, which ordered lectionary revision for the Roman Catholic Church:

> The treasures of the Bible are to be opened up more lavishly, so that richer fare may be provided for the faithful at the table of God's Word. In this way a more representative portion of the holy Scriptures will be read to the people over a set cycle of years. (*The Documents of Vatican II*, Walter Abbott, ed. [Piscataway, N.J.: New Century, 1974], p. 155)

The example thus set by the Roman Catholics inspired the Protestants to take more seriously the place of the Bible in their services and sermons, and soon many denominations had issued their own three-year cycles, based generally on the Roman Catholic model but with their own modifications. This explains why some discrepancies and variations appear in different forms of the lectionary. The Revised Common Lectionary (RCL) is an effort to increase agreement among the churches. A table at the end of the volume will list the differences between the RCL and the Roman Catholic, Episcopal, and Lutheran lectionaries. Where no entry is made for the latter, their use accords with the RCL.

For those unacquainted with the general pattern of the lectionary, a brief word of explanation may be helpful for sermon preparation. (1) The three years are each distinguished by one of the Synoptic Gospels: Matthew in A, Mark in B, Luke in C. John is distributed over the three years with a heavy emphasis during Lent and Easter. (2) Two types of readings are used. During the periods of Advent to Epiphany and Lent to Pentecost, the readings are usually topical—that is, there is some common theme among them. During the Sundays after Epiphany and Pentecost the readings are continuous, with no necessary connection between the lessons. In the period covered by this volume, there is a thematic connection for Trinity Sunday, but the rest of the Sundays follow continuous Old Testament (Samuel and Kings), epistle (II Corinthians and Ephesians), and Gospel (Mark and John) tracks. The Old Testament readings are from the Davidic narrative in recognition of Mark's concern to present Jesus as the Son of David. In II Corinthians we find Paul defending his ministry and in so doing providing many texts that will serve to help a congregation explore the meaning of its own ministry. Ephesians then explores what it means to be the community of the Church, made one in Christ, whose ministry we are about. These are bold, general themes, and are intended to provide a theological environment for homiletical thought rather than a thematic outline between all three lessons from week to week.

Perhaps it should also be added that although the psalm is intended to be a response by the people to the Old Testament lesson—rather than being read as a lesson on its own—that in no way suggests that it cannot be used as the text for the sermon.

In addition to this twelve-volume series, Abingdon Press also offers the following resources to supplement your work with the lectionary:

The Revised Common Lectionary is the work of the Consultation on Common Texts. It contains the complete listing for all three years of the lectionary, plus two helpful indexes listing passages by sequence in the Bible and by the order of the Christian year.

The Lectionary Bible is based upon the New Revised Standard Version of the Bible and contains the printed texts of all three years for the Revised Common Lectionary.

Living with the Lectionary: Preaching Through the Revised Common Lectionary by Eugene Lowry is a guide to the benefits and liabilities of preaching on lectionary texts.

Litanies and Other Prayers for the Revised Common Lectionary, by Everett Tilson and Phyllis Cole, is a three-volume anthology of prayers, calls to worship, and responses that are inspired by the weekly texts.

Forbid Them Not is a three-volume commentary based on the lectionary by Carolyn Brown, which is specifically aimed at the children in the congregation. A worship handout for each week is provided.

SUMMER SUNDAY PREACHING IN PENTECOST

Few preachers seem to look forward to that long expanse of
Sundays reaching from Trinity Sunday to Labor Day. It is a time
for planning what will happen after Labor Day and for making
vacation plans. Father's Day, the Fourth, and Labor Day
Sunday are not high holy days on the calendars of most local
churches, and at most provide blips on the liturgical screen.
Indeed, two months intervene between Independence Day and
Labor Day, and the preacher's imagination is taxed to find ways
in which to make service and sermon "meaningful." This
creative breakdown has been known to result in various kinds of
experimental and innovative liturgies and sermons—which, if
they fail, make no one feel too badly because they were in the
nature of a trial balloon, an attention getter, after all. They
perhaps provide the best justification for defining the liturgy as
that which is intended to save the people of God from the
pastor's bright ideas!

Into this dilemma comes the lectionary as a means of
introducing what might seem to be a revolutionary concept in
many places, that of reading, studying, and celebrating the
scriptural witness in a consecutive way over a sustained period
of time. The key here is the word *consecutive* and appreciating
why it is necessary to understand the overall structure of the
lectionary.

During the "proper" times of the year, Advent to Epiphany
and Ash Wednesday to Pentecost, the lessons are generally
chosen so as to have some kind of thematic connection, drawing
together varied scriptural witnesses to help us gain insight into

the meaning of the sacred mystery being anticipated or celebrated. Volumes 1 and 2 in this series illustrate that pattern. Even the "ordinary" Sundays between Epiphany and Ash Wednesday have the Old Testament lessons chosen in relation to the day's Gospel which, with the epistle, is being read sequentially. But when we come to the ordinary time after Pentecost, the lessons operate on three independent tracks with no intentional thematic relationship between them.

In Year B, the ruling Gospel is Mark, the evangelist who is particularly concerned with portraying Jesus as the Son of David. The Old Testament lessons after Pentecost then are chosen from the Davidic cycle to complement Mark's interest. They begin with the story of the boy Samuel—who, as prophet, will anoint David king in succession to Saul and conclude with the accession of David's son Solomon. Because of the tradition concerning the wisdom of Solomon, the later lessons of the time are taken from the wisdom literature. The intent is not that there be a one-on-one thematic connection between the two readings; it is rather that the Old Testament lessons provide us with the context and tradition within which Mark was thinking and writing. The epistle lessons throughout the summer months are from II Corinthians, a volume in which Paul struggles to explain what it means to be involved in a ministry that is based upon the cross, which for Mark is central to understanding the work of the Anointed One.

The mention of the three-fold set of lessons provides occasion to discuss the order of the reading of the lessons. The intent of the lectionary is that the order be Old Testament, psalm response, epistle, Gospel. The psalm is a response to the Old Testament reading, not a lesson in itself (though that does not mean it cannot be used as the text for the sermon, since it is a part of the canon). This use of the psalter as a resource for prayer and praise reminds us of our roots in synagogue and Temple. In the epistle we hear the apostolic witness, which understands itself to be in continuity with the work of God in the experience of Israel in the Old Testament and sees itself as a fulfillment of God's promise to Israel. The Gospel is read last, because that is the vehicle through which the community interprets both the experience of Israel and the primitive Church. There is a kind of historical development here, since usually each reading is older in time than the one following it, but this is no justification for the pattern. The rationale is unabashedly christological. It is through Christ that we view and interpret both the witness of the Old Testament and the apostles. It is for this reason that in many traditions the congregation stands to hear the Gospel read—not because the Gospels are somehow "better" scripture, but because they are an icon of Christ in our midst, and it is Christ whom we stand to greet.

This means that the order of the lessons is not changed so that the one with the primary text is closest to the sermon, because we still need the word of Christ through which to focus our attention. Even if, in ordinary time, the Gospel does not relate thematically to either of the previous lessons, it is still the last lesson because of the symbolic lesson to be learned. It may be that there is a particular Gospel lesson that the preacher has used as a vehicle for interpreting one of the earlier lessons. That may provide a justification for changing the Gospel of the day in order to establish the thematic connection. For example, Proper 14 has as the Old Testament lesson the story of the death of Absalom and David's subsequent grief. The Gospel is part of Jesus' discourse in John 6 about being the bread of life, a rich mine for preaching, but which may be difficult to relate to Absalom hanging by his hair from a tree limb! This preacher might exercise personal freedom to change the Gospel for the day to Matthew 23:37-39, Jesus' lament over Jerusalem, in order to compare the grief of David and David's great Son. Nothing is lost from Mark, since today's Gospel is from John, which might be included next week, and the lament narrative is not included in the readings from Matthew in Year A. The epistle for the day is part of the ethical teaching at the end of Ephesians. It certainly can stand on its own as a separate reading, but it may be related to the other two lessons in terms of the basis for ethical action, which is expressed by the fact that "God in Christ has forgiven you" (4:32). That forgiveness (at what cost to God!) moves us from rebellion and slayers of the prophets to those who, sealed by the Spirit, are engaged in "what is useful for building up."

This kind of creative and critical thinking allows for an expansion of the lectionary by the insightful preacher if each set is taken in turn each three years as the governing lesson. The preacher then makes other thematic choices (assuming that the integrity of the texts is maintained). Already one's preaching ministry has developed possibilities for the next nine years, and it mitigates the accusation that the lectionary limits the preacher's choice of texts.

In recent years, the dictum that the text and the sermon should not be separated has become a kind of mantra that has given rise to a new liturgical legalism that does not understand the liturgical setting out of which the dictum originated. The reason for the rule is not to disallow a hymn between lesson and sermon (or even two lessons with responses). It grows out of the practice, still current in some places, of having the (one and only) Scripture lesson very early on in the service, followed by a pastoral prayer, an anthem, the offering, the announcements, a hymn, and whatever else, and then finally the sermon. That is the kind of separation the rule is intended to prevent.

Perhaps most important for the preacher is to remember that though it may be called "ordinary" time, it is still *kairos* with which we are dealing, and that for the Christian time is always a means of grace. Ideally, the lectionary intends that there be a convergence of the Word of the Lord with the Supper of the Lord on the Day of the Lord. The dismemberment of these in practice has led to a diminished identity on the part of the Christian community. The Word without the Supper becomes as breath without body, because it denies the incarnational principle enunciated in John 1, which is at the heart of the Christian revelation. No less tragic is the celebration of the Supper without the proclamation of the Word, which gives us a body without breath. And equally tragic is the confusion of the Sabbath with the Lord's Day. It has been found easier to observe the Sabbath with its negations than to live with the scandalous joy and grace that characterize life in the kingdom.

Our understanding of Sunday has to do with our understanding of Easter, for it is responsible for the whole enterprise called the Christian Church. Easter is the formative event for Christians, the eighth day of the new creation, the day which reminds us that we have died, been buried, and raised with Christ, and as a result our view of the world will henceforth be slightly skewed, because we are learning to look at life from the other side of the Resurrection. Proper time is rather straightforward as we hear again the ancient narratives, remember "the old, old story," and rejoice at our incorporation into the mighty acts of God. But ordinary time is no time to act as though all of that never happened! On the contrary, ordinary time is the setting for applying Easter to make life extraordinary. Second Corinthians and Ephesians can give us a model this summer (as can other Pauline letters). Ephesians concludes as a study in ethics with that most significant "So then" at 4:25 (epistle for Proper 14). The question always before us during ordinary time is, What do we do about Easter? The lessons suggest resources in our search for answers. A strictly Sabbatarian view of the day will incline us toward legalisms and social securities in our ethics; the Lord who picks corn on the Sabbath will have something to say to us about what it means to have his life "made visible in our mortal flesh" as we both receive the sacrament and become the sacrament for the world (Proper 4).

The former pattern for counting the days in the Christian year always spoke of days "After Pentecost" or "After Trinity," and the tendency then was to think of that time as "the season of Pentecost." Both lectionary and calendar reform have recovered the primitive understanding that the Day of Pentecost is part of Easter, the Great Fifty Days, and that resurrection and empowerment by the Spirit are inseparable (see commentary in Year A, Lent/Easter of this series). We live empowered by the Spirit of the risen Christ, and "so then," we are now about the business of seeking the things that are above, and that has implications for how we go about the business of living here below. The preacher's exciting challenge this and every summer is to engage the congregation in dialogue about what it means to love God and do as you please!

The standard color for ordinary time is green. To avoid tedium and monotony during these six months, a variety of greens and summer colors (e.g., red-orange) might be used along with fresh flowers from local gardens. The lessons for the day may also present ideas for different kinds of visuals from Sunday to Sunday.

Trinity Sunday (First Sunday After Pentecost)

Old Testament Texts

Isaiah 6 describes the call of Isaiah in the Jerusalem Temple. Psalm 29 is a hymn praising God through the imagery of the thunderstorm. The call of Isaiah is also featured during Epiphany in Year C.

The Lesson: *Isaiah 6:1-8*

Holiness and Atonement

Setting. A sermon on Isaiah 6 might focus on two features of the setting for this text. First, it includes features of a prophetic call, and thus participates in the formal aspects of this genre, although the emphasis on a heavenly vision in Isaiah 6 is a rare element (see also I Kings 22:19). Prophetic call narratives tend to follow a six-part sequence of action that consists of divine confrontation, introductory word, commission, objection, reassurance, and sign. (See the commentary on Exodus 3:1-15 for Year A, Proper 17 and on Judges 6:1-12 for Year A, Proper 27 for further discussion of call narratives.) Second, the setting of the call of Isaiah is clearly the Jerusalem Temple; the imagery picks up many aspects of the architecture and liturgy of the Temple. Note, for example, the enthronement language attributed to God in relationship to the altar in v. 1, the seraphs that surround the divine throne on the altar to form a heavenly council in v. 2, liturgical chanting in v. 3, and incense (smoke) in v. 4. The combination of prophetic call and the setting of the sanctuary provide an occasion to explore holiness and its two-sided effect on profane humans—death or atonement.

Structure. If the prophetic call of Isaiah is emphasized to the congregation, then the boundaries of the text should be expanded to include the whole chapter. All aspects of the prophetic call, however, do not appear in the passage (there is no sign). Verses 1-7 constitute the divine confrontation and introductory word, which in the case of Isaiah is a vision in the Jerusalem Temple. The commission is in the form of a divine question in v. 8*a* that the prophet overhears. This is a departure from the expected form where God normally states a direct command to an individual (see, for example, Moses or Gideon), which then prompts objection by the one being called. Isaiah's call is playing with this expected form in two ways. First, as noted, he overhears a divine question rather than receiving a direct command. Second, having just survived a near-death experience (seeing God and still living), he is overly motivated and volunteers to be sent out, when the expected form tells us that he should have objected. Isaiah then receives his commission, which is paradoxical. He must preach to confirm blindness in the people. In v. 11 the prophet realizes what he has gotten himself into and musters an objection, "How long O Lord?" The answer: until destruction is complete. The prophetic call of Isaiah is to confirm the guilt of Israel and thus seal their destruction, much like a manager who is hired for the sole purpose of shutting down a factory.

The lectionary text focuses on Isaiah rather than the literary features of his call. And in particular the event of theophany, the danger of divine holiness for him, his realization of it, and his experience of atonement. Here the text separates into the vision (vv. 1-2), liturgy (vv. 3-4), the prophet's recognition of danger (v. 5), and his atonement (vv. 6-8).

Significance. The root meaning of *holiness* is "separation." When holiness is attributed to God in the Bible, we understand that God is separate from our everyday world. This notion has been carried through into more contemporary theology with the concept of God's "otherness." The distinction between the sacred and the profane arises from a recognition that God is holy and hence separate from our everyday profane lives. Sin is central to the concept of God's separateness. But sin in this case is more like the notion of pollution than specific human actions, even though human action might have prompted the pollution in the first place. The result of our actions is that we and our everyday world are polluted, and, furthermore, we have evolved in such a way that we actually need a polluted environment to maintain our lives. God, on the other hand, is not polluted and hence is fundamentally separate from us and our world. One can see here how holiness could prompt a very "otherworldly" religion. But that is not the case in ancient Israel. Instead, Israel confessed that the holy (and separate) God did not abandon this polluted world but entered back into it by being enthroned in the Temple. Such mixing of a pure God and a polluted world is dangerous because the two are not compatible. Thus the holiness of God is dangerous for anyone and anything in the profane world, and the Temple with its liturgy is meant to provide a means by which the dangerous presence of God can be channeled safely into our world.

The dynamic tension and danger between the sacred and the profane is central for interpreting Isaiah 6:1-8. Notice how the distance (or separateness) between the holy God and the profane prophet is maintained in the opening verses. Although the prophet sees the enthroned God, it is only the hem of the divine robe that actually enters the Temple. Furthermore, the prophet hardly catches a glimpse of God before the focus changes to intermediary divine beings, the Seraphim, who are themselves separate from God. These winged creatures, perhaps like cobra snakes with wings, cover their faces and their feet, while they sing:

"Holy, holy, holy is the Lᴏʀᴅ of hosts;
the whole earth is full of his glory."

The content of the hymn goes to the heart of Israel's understanding of God. The first line underscores God's separateness, while the second line proclaims his presence. This is a dangerous situation, which the prophet immediately recognizes, " 'Woe is me: I am lost, for I am a man of unclean lips, and I live among a people of unclean lips.' " Note how sin in this case is pollution (uncleanness).

Fire is one of the central motifs in ancient Israel for conveying the danger that exists when the holy God enters our profane world. The motif enters the text in v. 6 through the image of a burning coal. Fire is so often associated with the holy because it is two-sided and hence dangerous: It can destroy or purify. This two-sided action is played out in the larger call of Isaiah. In the case of the prophet, the fire of divine presence purifies him. His pollution is decontaminated, or to use the words of the text: "Your guilt has departed and your sin is blotted out." In the case of the people of Israel it will lead to total destruction through a bonfire (vv. 9b-13, see especially, v. 13 "Even if a tenth part remain in it, it will be burned again . . .").

Isaiah 6 provides a springboard for exploring the themes of divine separateness, sin as pollution, and salvation as atonement. The contemporary church, however, has fashioned a casual approach to God. Central images today include mother, father, friend, or companion on a journey. A strong biblical base is apparent for each of these images, but God is never a casual presence. The holiness or otherness of God needs to be proclaimed in the contemporary church, and our ever increasing awareness of environmental pollution provides an excellent background for exploring the separateness of God from our world.

The Response: *Psalm 29*

A Hymn of Praise

Setting. Psalm 29 is a powerful hymn of praise. It celebrates the rule of God over nature through the motifs of a storm. The frequent repetition of "the voice of the Lord" (seven times in vv. 3-9) is best interpreted as thunder, which is accompanying a storm that has rolled off the Mediterranean Sea and is hitting the coast, from there it shakes the cedars of Lebanon in the north, before it swings southward to cast bolts of lightning in the southern wilderness of Kadesh. The imagery is vivid and ancient. Scholars have traced many of these motifs, which celebrate the power of God in and over nature, to the Canaanite culture that preceded Israel. Some scholars cite evidence that this hymn may even have been a hymn to Ba'al the storm god before it was refashioned into a song about Yahweh.

Structure. Psalm 29 follows the structure of a hymn, and thus it separates into three parts: an introduction in vv. 1-2, which functions as a call to praise; an enumeration of the praiseworthy acts of God in vv. 3-9; and a conclusion in vv. 10-11, which both gives reasons why God should be praised while it also calls the worshiper once again to praise God. The hymn is tightly woven in its construction. For example, the introduction and conclusion balance each other with four lines, while each also refers to "the Lord" four times.

Significance. Psalm 29 is a celebration of divine power in this world, and as such it functions well as an extension of the call of Isaiah. Whereas the call of Isaiah emphasized the separateness of God and need for atonement, Psalm 29 probes the presence of God. But again we should note how the images are not casual and how ultimately the worshiper is encouraged to look for God in worship rather than nature. Note how the introduction calls the community to worship (vv. 1-2) while the conclusion assures them of God's power in their midst (vv. 10-11).

New Testament Texts

The texts for Trinity Sunday bring together two dynamic, but quite different, passages—both of which reflect upon the vital role and work of the Spirit in the formation of divinely reformed life. Paul ponders the Spirit's reformation of life as the cause for Christian hope, and in John, Jesus reasons about the absolute necessity of transformation by the Spirit for true life.

The Epistle: *Romans 8:12-17*

Life in the Spirit as Life of Hope

Setting. Within the larger section of Romans 5–8 the eighth chapter is itself a nearly self-contained unity with clearly identifiable parts. Generally this chapter is a meditation on the nature and significance of Christian life. This reflection functions in two crucial ways for Paul's letter. First, this section "ends" Paul's long reflection on the operation of grace in chapters 5–8. Second, this beautiful, hopeful meditation immediately precedes the following agonizing section of Romans, chapters 9–11, which will wrestle with the fate of Israel in the working of God's grace.

Structure. Chapter 8 is neatly structured. Verses 1-11 take up the theme of Christian life as life in the Spirit. Then, vv. 12-17 employ the metaphors of sonship (obscured in the NRSV) and childhood (preserved and amplified to take in sonship in the NRSV) to reflect upon the significance of our relationship to God. Next, vv. 18-30 bring a strong eschatological cast to Paul's thought by speaking of future freedom and glory. Finally, vv. 31-39 conclude this section by declaring the ultimate destiny of Christian life to be victory through "the love of God in Christ Jesus our Lord."

Significance. Following Paul closely through the careful sections of chapter 8, especially vv. 12-17 , is not easy work. The opening words, "So then," let us know that Paul is drawing conclusions from the previous verses where he made the clear positive point that Christian life is life in the Spirit, not life in the flesh or under the law of sin. Verses 12-17 give the "because" for vv. 1-11. To paraphrase: Christian life is life in the Spirit because persons led by the Spirit are the children of God. In one way Paul is speaking about Christian identity or self-understanding (more communal than individual, though there are implications for individuals); but, he goes on to speak about the significance of such life. Life in the Spirit is much more than an identity; indeed it is a relationship to God, which has come as a gift from God. For now, the distance between (sinful) humanity and (righteous) God is overcome as God adopts us as God's children. And Paul continues. Since we are now God's children, we will be heirs. This expansion of the metaphor accomplishes at least two things: (1) It introduces a profound eschatological cast to the meditation—we are experiencing grace, and there is more to come! (2) It translates Christian suffering into meaningful suffering. If we are co-heirs with Christ, Paul says our suffering for Christ (he is not talking about routine health or financial problems) is like Christ's own suffering—that is, an anticipation of the glory to which God will bring us.

Having registered the motifs of life, the Spirit, relationship to God, eschatology, Christ, and suffering before the Romans (vv. 1-17), Paul speeds up his argument by moving into a new gear (vv. 18-30). His topic is life in the Spirit as a life of hope. Paul focused on the community of Roman (and other?) Christians in vv. 1-17; and those remarks function as a springboard to the articulation of his vision of the cosmic scope of the operation of grace through the work of the Spirit. Paul's line of reasoning is difficult, because we are neither adept at thinking in such cosmic terms nor really accustomed to reflecting upon the need of redemption for creation. Yet, the apostle works with a deep conviction that the very fabric of creation is itself, like humankind, captive to the corrupting power of sin, so that creation, or the cosmos, is at odds with

God; but Paul also believes and states that "the creation itself will be set free from its bondage to decay and will obtain the freedom of the glory of the children of God." In Paul's vision of God's work of redemption, humanity and the cosmos are intricately related to each other. The fate of one is the fate of the other. Why? Because humanity and the cosmos have in common that they are creatures, created by the one creator, God. The hope of all creation is in the faithful creator who did not abandon a sin-trapped creation, but in Jesus Christ reclaimed and thoroughly identified with all of creation. Thus Paul can make the bold statement found in Romans 8.

The Gospel: *John 3:1-17*

The Necessity of Second Birth

Setting. We come on Trinity Sunday to another text from the early portions of the Fourth Gospel. This text gives us a section of the story of Jesus' encounter with Nicodemus (3:1-21). The passage is filled with unique Johannine thoughts, language, ideas, and literary techniques.

Structure. John begins with a narrative (3:1-2*a*) which rapidly turns into a conversation (3:2*b*-11) and eventuates in Jesus' making a speech (3:12-21). The conversation runs through three cycles: First, Nicodemus makes a statement that Jesus "answers" (oddly) with a declaration about second birth; and Nicodemus asks, "How . . . ?" (vv. 2*b*-4). Second, Jesus gives another pronouncement-answer about second birth; and Nicodemus queries, "How . . . ?" (vv. 5-9). Third, Jesus responds with a question and an elaborate statement about "earthly things" and "heavenly things" and God's saving love, which motivated the sending of God's Son to save the world (vv. 10-17 [21]).

Significance. In John's storytelling Nicodemus functions as a kind of straight man for Jesus. This whole incident is crafted in one of John's favorite forms: a narrative introduces dialogue that produces misunderstanding which allows Jesus to make a long speech. Indeed, in the initial exchanges between Jesus and Nicodemus, Jesus addresses Nicodemus with the singular form of the second person pronoun, *you*; but beginning in v. 12, Jesus suddenly starts to speak to you all—employing the second person plural pronoun. Nicodemus simply disappears in the narrative after he speaks in v. 9 and is addressed by Jesus in vv. 10-11. Clearly the story and the conversation are pointed toward a larger audience that is directly addressed (you all) in vv. 12-17 (21).

The scene is highly symbolic. Nicodemus comes "by night"—at least as much a reference to his being in the dark as it is to the time of day. The conversation refers to (1) "signs"—an interpretation of the nature and purpose of Jesus' mighty acts (or miracles); (2) being born *anōthen*—an ambiguous Greek word that can mean "again" or "from above"; (3) being "born of water and the Spirit"—namely, divine cleansing in the messianic age; (4) "wind and the Spirit"—a word play evoking images of divine creative activity; (5) Jesus' being "lifted up"—a complex reference to Jesus' crucifixion and exaltation; and (6) "eternal life"—a qualitative, not merely, durative existence in relation to God. Moreover, throughout the larger passage there is a steady stream of antinomic apocalyptic language: flesh/Spirit (v. 6), earth/heaven (v. 12), light/darkness (v. 13), believing/not believing (v. 18), and doing evil/doing truth (v. 21).

Poor Nicodemus follows nearly none of this! Rather, the befuddled Nicodemus is confronted at every state of his inquiry by ambiguous metaphors and enigmatic antinomies that contrast the human and the divine, so that his initial claims to knowledge and belief are frustrated, if not refuted. The episode reveals that Nicodemus knows nothing other than that Jesus came from God, and that knowledge alone is inadequate. Yet, this is more a literary device than a historical recollection. Indeed, as Nicodemus does not comprehend, Jesus speaks more and more so that we the readers of the Gospel are in the privileged position of being instructed by Jesus on a series of topics.

The first cycle of conversation declares the necessity of divinely empowered spiritual birth. Jesus says one must be born *anōthen,* and Nicodemus hears "again" rather than "from above," so that his subsequent remarks are comical, but we get the point. The second cycle elaborates the theme, teaching that entry into God's kingdom requires divinely empowered spiritual birth because like answers to like; thus, without the movement of the Spirit in our lives we have no means of relating to God. The third cycle clarifies the role of Jesus in salvation: At God's initiative, because of God's love, God sent or gave God's Son, who is the criterion of salvation. The presence and person of Jesus Christ forces a crisis, so that Jesus is the catalyst that precipitates a separation of "light" and "darkness," of "truth" and "evil."

The passage makes a profound statement, highly relevant for our lives. Orthodoxy is not the key to being a Christian; rather, God expects an inseparable bonding of orthodoxy and orthopraxis. Eternal life is a quality of existence that has its beginning in this life in anticipation of another life. Eternal life came because of what God has done in Jesus Christ. Christians live out of a belief that Jesus guides and empowers all of existence.

Trinity Sunday: The Celebration

Ordinary time is always bracketed by special days, whether after Epiphany or Pentecost. After Epiphany they are the Baptism of the Lord and the Transfiguration. After Pentecost they are Trinity Sunday and Christ the King.

Trinity Sunday represents both a summing up of the divine activity, which we have been celebrating since the beginning of Advent, and a reminder of the whole work and being of

God—in creation, redemption, and sanctification—which is still ongoing and which provides the context for our life of celebration, witness, and service throughout the rest of ordinary time. While the other days of the calendar commemorate events in salvation history, Trinity Sunday—for Protestants anyway is the only day devoted to a doctrine or an article of faith. Even among the Roman Catholics it was a late arrival on the liturgical scene, not being required of all churches until the fourteenth century.

Because the doctrine of the Trinity is derived from the cumulative witness of the scriptural revelation, preachers will seek in vain for any one text to serve as a basis for expounding the mystery. Today's epistle and Gospel lessons can only provide data for discussing the work of the Persons of the Trinity, but by themselves they cannot prove the doctrine. Texts need to enter into dialogue with one another for the fullness of the doctrine to emerge. The goal of preaching on this day is not to seek intellectual assent to a doctrinal formulation, or even to make clear what the doctrine means (if a preacher can in fact do that without falling into one of the multiple brands of Trinitarian heresy). Rather, Trinitarian preaching should seek to re-create in the hearers those experiences of God above us, God among us, and God within us, which have led theologians to their conclusions. Preaching and theological lecturing, like the Trinity, participate in the same reality but have different manifestations!

The use of Isaiah 6 is only typologically related to the Trinity because of the Ter-Sanctus sung by the seraphs, and it witnesses to the mystery of God who condescends to self-disclosure in the experience of the worshiper. The experience is not induced by the worshiper or the worship leader; it is a divine action initiated by God. The use of this text on this day suggests such hymns as "Holy, Holy, Holy" and "Holy God, We Praise Thy Name." The following prayer has been adapted from the former Roman mass where it was said by priest or deacon before the reading of

the Gospel. In this form it may be used as a Prayer for
Illumination.

> Cleanse our hearts and our lips, O almighty God,
> as you cleansed the lips of the prophet Isaiah
> with a burning coal,
> so that we may worthily proclaim and hear
> your holy Word;
> through Christ our Lord. Amen.

Proper Four
Sunday Between
May 29 and June 4 Inclusive
(If After Trinity Sunday)

Old Testament Texts

First Samuel 3 is the account of Samuel's call in the Temple, while Psalm 139:1-6, 13-18 is a hymn of praise.

The Lesson: *I Samuel 3:1-10 (11-20)*

God's Initiative

Setting. The Song of Hannah in I Samuel 2:1*b*-8 provides an introduction to the thematic and structural development for I and II Samuel. A brief look at this hymn will provide background for reading the lectionary text. The book opens with a conflict between Hannah, who is barren, and Peninnah, who has many children. This story is familiar and can be summarized quickly. Hannah goes to Shiloh and prays for a child at the sanctuary where Eli is priest. Her request is for a son, which God grants in the birth of Samuel. Hannah's song celebrates the power of God to answer prayer and to initiate salvation. The content of her song is very important, for she describes the power of God to initiate salvation as radical reversals in life. God can bring the arrogant low and break the bows of the mighty (vv. 2-4*a*), and, conversely, he can strengthen the weak and feed the hungry (vv. 4*b*-5*a*). Finally, Hannah celebrates the reversal in her own life by recounting God's power to make a barren woman pregnant (v. 5*b*). The song underscores how God's ability to initiate salvation is a two-sided sword: "he brings low, he also exalts" (v. 7*b*). The thematic development of I and II Samuel is in many ways an illustration of Hannah's song. Characters are frequently paired in contrasting situations so that while one is on the rise, another is on the decline (Peninnah-Hannah, Eli [and his son]-Samuel, Samuel [and his son]-Saul, Saul [and his son]-David, and so on). This structure provides background for reading the call of Samuel in I Samuel 3.

Structure. The interrelationship of characters is central to the story, and, for that reason, it is important to include the larger boundaries of the lectionary text, vv. 1-20. The text separates into four parts: vv. 1-3 provide an introduction and setting, vv. 4-9 are an introductory word for the call of Samuel, vv. 10-15 are the account of God's revelation, and vv. 16-20 provide the conclusion. Note how the story begins (vv. 1-3) and ends (vv. 16-20) with Eli and Samuel, while the two middle sections focus primarily on Samuel and God.

Significance. The central focus for the lectionary is God's initiative. The call of Samuel is a good choice for this Sunday, because it adds complexity to our very easy confessions about God's initiative in our lives, especially during good times. More specifically, it is the character of Eli that adds complexity to the story, and our interpretation will focus on the important (and ambiguous) role that he plays in bringing the call of Samuel to a proper conclusion.

As noted, Samuel and Eli frame the story of I Samuel 3. We should also note, however, that by the time we reach the conclusion their roles are reversed. In the introduction we are told that Samuel is a mere boy and that he is serving Eli. Furthermore, we learn that although God is removed ("the word of the LORD was rare in those days"), he is not completely absent, because of Eli ("Eli's eyesight is dim . . . but the lamp of God had not yet gone out.''). This statement in vv. 2-3 has several functions in the larger story. On the one hand the reference to dimness prepares us for the rise of Samuel and the fall of Eli. On the other hand, it makes Eli an ambiguous character, because he still has "sight." The earlier chapter introduced this ambiguity concerning Eli through the story of his worthless sons (2:22-25). Yet Eli is not his sons, and even though they reflect a flaw in him, he is still a priest of God. This situation raises the question of how he will act in his own decline.

God enters the story in the two middle sections. In good storytelling fashion God addresses Samuel three times (vv. 4-9) before the boy understands his own clairvoyance the fourth time (vv. 10-15). We can read these sections as the call of Samuel, and if we do so, the story illustrates the power of God to initiate salvation even to a child. But such a reading is too simplistic, because it is the dim vision of Eli that is the real catalyst for God's initiative. Note how in v. 7 we are explicitly told that Samuel did not know God. Then in v. 8 it is Eli who perceives the call of God, and in v. 9 he tutors the boy on how to respond to God. Eli's tutoring of Samuel allows the revelation in vv. 10-15 to take place, which, paradoxically, is a judgment against Eli. The judgment is so severe that the ears of anyone who hears it will actually tingle (v. 11, see also II Kings 21:12 and Habakkuk 3:16 for further discussion of "tingling" because of divine judgment).

God is once again absent in the conclusion. It begins in v. 15 with the relationship between Samuel and Eli unchanged. Samuel fears to convey the message, but Eli exerts his authority by invoking a potential divine curse on the boy (v. 17). Thus Samuel capitulates and tells the priest of his downfall. Eli is given the final words of this exchange ("It is the Lord; let him do what seems good to him"), before he exits the story altogether, signifying the reversal in the roles between Samuel and Eli.

This is an insightful story for preaching on the topic of God's initiative, for it complicates the matter. To focus exclusively on the call of Samuel in I Samuel 3 runs the danger of being too romantic. The call of God then becomes an illustration of good things happening to good people. In preaching this text it is important to show how this text also addresses the grey and ambiguous world of Eli, wherein we find the real challenge of confessing God's power, when it may imply an admission of our own downfall. Biblical writers have underscored this point by making Eli such an important character in the call of Samuel, who will take Eli's place within several chapters.

The Response: *Psalm 139:1-6, 13-18*

A Hymn of Praise

Setting. The description of Psalm 139 in the heading as a hymn of praise is in fact not so clear. There is a didactic or wisdom quality to Psalm 139, in which the psalmist appears to teach those around her about the omnipresence of God, while the end of the psalm actually becomes a lament. The reason for designating the psalm as a hymn is to avoid the danger of reading this litany of divine power and presence as though it were impersonal. The content of the psalm arises out of the experience of the psalmist, which makes the statement about the absolute control of God over all time and space a source of praise. This is not a psalm that explores the dialectic of freedom and necessity.

Structure. The larger structure of Psalm 139 separates into two parts: vv. 1-18 are a hymn, and vv. 19-24 are a lament. The mood between these two sections is so sharp that a number of scholars have argued for two separated psalms. This may in fact be the case. The only problem with this conclusion is the close tie between vv. 1 and 23.

Verses 1-18 separate into three parts: vv. 1-6 are a confession of how intimately God knows the psalmist, vv. 7-12 reflect on the omnipresence of God through creation, while vv. 13-18 continue the reflection by moving to the more intimate metaphors of how God was present in the creation of the psalmist. The lectionary text is limited to the first and third parts.

Significance. The clue to reading this hymn is found in the combination of vv. 7-12 and 13-18. Verses 7-12 underscore how God is everywhere, by showing how the psalmist cannot escape the spirit in either heaven or hell (vv. 7-8), in the furthermost reaches of the earth (vv. 9-10), or even through magical incantations of conjuring up darkness (vv. 11-12). Such conceptions of omnipresence could be terrifying, but what makes them a springboard for praise is the change in the direction of images from the outer reaches of cosmology in vv. 7-12 to the intimacy of creating the psalmist in vv. 13-18. The imagery of God's presence in the privacy of the mother's womb in v. 13 may be anatomical, but it is more likely a reference to the earth. Note how v. 15 continues the imagery of v. 13 and explicitly states that the place of secret formation is the depths of the earth. In either case the point of this imagery is that the omnipresence of God is at the very origin of our creation. God has even beheld our unformed substance (v. 16), hence there is really nothing left to hide. The psalmist concludes from this that God's presence is not something to be avoided or feared but embraced, even when we cannot imagine how, or in what ways, our life's journey interweaves with God (v. 18). And, indeed, this confession provides an introduction to the psalm in vv. 1-6. One is reminded at the end of this psalm of Eli and his closing comments in I Samuel 3:18: "It is the Lord; let him do what seems good to him."

New Testament Texts

The texts for this week are the first of several sequential readings from II Corinthians and Mark as we return to "ordinary time." The discussion below of the setting (and, to a degree, structure) will serve as introductory material for the following weeks' lessons. In the epistle, Paul strives to inform the Corinthians about the true nature of discipleship—that is, life in relation to the true subject of the gospel, Jesus Christ. Mark recounts a series of controversy stories, all of which are told to underscore Jesus' authority and the radically new and striking character of his activity.

The Epistle: *II Corinthians 4:5-12*

The Treasure in Clay Jars

Setting. Sometime after Paul wrote I Corinthians, a group of outsiders arrived in Corinth. These people were Christian preachers, but their message was that Christianity was a vitally renewed Judaism wherein certain people possess the power to work miracles. These preachers claimed to possess that extraordinary power. Indeed, they maintained that they were sources of divine power. Paul referred to these people as "super-apostles," a clearly sarcastic designation in the apostle's use, but a title that may have been their self-designation. Although the super-apostles clearly came from Jewish Christian circles, they were like other Hellenistic religious propagandists of that day who had a flashy, obviously powerful style of ministry—powerful in proclamation and powerful in deeds.

There are distinguishable sections to II Corinthians. The recognizable portions of the letter are so distinct that many scholars conclude that the canonical letter is a later editor's compilation of preserved passages (fragments?) from more than one earlier letter. Whether or not this is the case, II Corinthians 2:14–7:4 is devoted to a defense of Paul's apostleship—namely, his ministry in word and deed.

Structure. Within II Corinthians 2:14–7:4 we find a section of introduction (2:14–3:6), a discussion proper of the substance and style of Paul's ministry (3:7–5:21), and a section of hortatory materials (6:1–7:4). As the paragraphing of the NRSV and most other modern translations shows, we join Paul in the middle of his argument at v. 5, and after his thought in progress is rounded off in v. 6, we continue to follow him into a new line of thought in vv. 7-12. Thus, there are two sections in the reading: Verses 5-6 articulate the nature of Paul's work in a quite blunt negative/positive juxtaposition of statements. Then, in a wealth of images and metaphors, vv. 7-12 define and interpret apostolic ministry as Paul understands it.

The logic of the reading is very suggestive for preaching. In v. 5, first, Paul states what he (or any other Christian) does not do; and, second, he declares what he (or, again, any other Christian) does. Verse 6 recognizes and declares the determinative nature of the work of God in and through Jesus Christ in the lives of Christians. Verses 7-12 "unpack" the practical meaning of Paul's theological perspective: It is precisely in human frailty that the true power of God is seen, for despite adversity that should shatter the human servant of God, the power of God makes itself known as the perishable human is preserved from destruction.

Significance. In the remarks of vv. 5-6 we learn that Paul does not consider himself the appropriate subject of Christian proclamation; rather, he preaches Christ as Lord. In the secondary level of the statement Paul locates himself in what he declares to be an appropriate Christian role—namely, in service to other believers for the sake of Jesus. Thus Paul maintains the priority of the Lord in ministry, but he shows that holding Jesus high means that one's interest in others will be greater than in oneself. Naming "Jesus" in this statement recalls the real human career of our Lord who lived a life of sacrificial self-giving. Paul concludes his thoughts in this part of the reading by declaring again that God is the source of his apostolic labors (similarly see 2:14, 17; 3:5-6; 4:1; and so on).

The NRSV (and NIV) alters the translation of the beginning of v. 7 to read, "But we have this treasure in clay jars," from the previous translation of the RSV which read, "But we have this treasure in earthen vessels.'' This new rendering is correct, but despite its employment of a more contemporary idiom, some of the romantic imagery of the old translation seems lost. Yet, perhaps this seeming loss is itself gain, for the beauty of the old idiom ran the danger of obscuring Paul's very point: As ''clay jars'' (the plural is deliberate and makes an important point concerning the shared condition of Christians) we believers are neither strikingly elegant nor powerfully secure. Paul's metaphor articulates a contrast between the finite humanity of believers and the infinite power of God. This distinction, Paul says, is necessary to make clear that God is the source of the power. Moreover, here the apostle argues that the power of God at work in human weakness is consistent with the paradoxical truth of the saving power of the Christ event.

Verse 7 is a thesis statement. It should be read and read again to assure that the point comes through clearly. Then, we see that vv. 8-9 are a series of contrasts demonstrating the sustaining power of God's grace. The key idea is that God's power is power that sustains those engaged in faithful service. Verses 10-12 articulate a kind of summary. They explicate, somewhat cryptically, Paul's basic point. A life of Christ-like service may well include Christ-like suffering, but believers may know that God's power sustains their efforts as God works through them to extend faith into the lives of others.

The Gospel: Mark 2:23–3:6

The Meaning of the Authority of Jesus

Setting. We last encountered this section of Mark in the readings for the Sundays after the Epiphany. The lesson for this week comes in the larger section, 2:1–3:35. There Mark records a series of controversy discourses and other stories. More specifically, in 2:1–3:6 we find a set of at least eight stories about Jesus' conflicts with religious authorities, and in these stories we see that Mark includes several authoritative pronouncements made by Jesus. Several key themes play in these accounts: The authority of Jesus to forgive sins, the freedom of Jesus in his choice of those among whom he works, the true character of Jesus' piety, the innovative nature of Jesus' ministry, and Jesus' attitude toward the Sabbath.

Structure. Our lesson for this Sunday falls into three parts. Mark 2:23-26 recounts the controversy around the picking of grain on the Sabbath; 2:27-28 records a pair of Sabbath sayings; and 3:1-6 tells the story of the healing of a man's hand on the Sabbath. Any one, two, or all three stories may serve as the text for preaching, for the individual parts are told in such a way that each may stand independently, but there are common concerns and themes that hold the materials together. In the following remarks we shall treat the parts of our lesson together and then separately.

Significance. Explicitly the verses of our lesson are statements about the authority of Jesus; implicitly they offer a critique of rigid religiosity and/or perverse piety. Mark's Gospel as a whole is a story about Jesus, about his identity as the Christ, or Messiah, or God's anointed one; it is also a story about Jesus as the Son of God. Knowing Jesus as God's Son is a crucial matter of faith for Mark. But Mark tells his story of Jesus in such a way that it is clear that to know who Jesus is as the Son of God is possible only as we understand him in terms of the concrete course of his ministry—up to and especially including his saving death on the cross. Merely knowing that Jesus is God's Son and, therefore, that he has authority is not enough for Mark. To understand Jesus clearly we must see and examine carefully how Jesus acted authoritatively. Through the stories and the remembrances of Jesus' sayings, Mark brings his readers into an encounter with this one whom he would have us to know.

Notice in the first story (vv. 23-26) that it is the disciples, not Jesus himself, who picked "heads of grain" on the Sabbath—although notice also that Jesus does not attempt to stop them. Furthermore, notice that Jesus' opponents, the

Pharisees, have taken a particular portion of Scripture and have read it in a particular manner, whereas Jesus defends his disciples by referring to another portion of Scripture and interpreting it in a different manner. The Pharisees focus on the Law, and they read it in literal fashion. Jesus focuses on the memories of Israel's history (specifically, here, David's time), and he applies it to his own time through analogy. The shape of the text, however, shows us that we have here more than a difference in hermeneutics. Mark's casting of the Pharisees seems stereotypical. We do not know historically that all Pharisees were so "legalistic," though we do know that their piety was regarded as exemplary by the majority of the Jewish people (themselves not Pharisees).

When we come to the third portion of our lesson, the story of the healing of a man's hand, we find the same basic attitude and approach on the part of the Pharisees. Now, however, Mark refers explicitly to their hostility toward Jesus. In an important way for Mark's Gospel this story (and the others of this section) sets the stage for the ultimate confrontation between Jesus and the religious authorities of Israel that brought on Jesus' execution—though we should not miss seeing that the Sadducees, not the Pharisees, are in league with the Romans in the course of Jesus' Passion.

The sayings in vv. 27-28 form a key to our interpretation of the lesson(s). Jesus operates with an assumption that God establishes norms and interacts with human beings for their good. God does not make rules to see whether we will comply. God wills the well-being of humanity, so that real human need, not rigid religion, determines the course of human existence. Jesus lived and revealed a God of love, and the authority he claimed and exercised bespoke God's ministry to humankind.

Proper 4: The Celebration

Today's lectionary leads us to two old hymns that may contribute to the liturgy through the use of single stanzas sung either by the choir or a solo voice.

As a call to worship, Psalm 139:17-18 might be read responsively, followed by the first stanza of "Still, Still with Thee" (*The Book of Hymns,* United Methodist [1964], no. 264; *Cokesbury Worship Hymnal,* no. 114; *The Hymnal,* Presbyterian [1933], no. 107; *Hymns for the Living Church,* no. 552).

At the conclusion of the service, Psalm 139:11-12 could also be read responsively, followed by the singing of the following arrangement of lines from the hymn, "Savior, Again to Thy Dear Name":

> Grant us thy peace upon our homeward way;
> with thee began, with thee shall end the day.
> From harm and danger keep thy children free,
> for dark and light are both alike to thee.

The formal benediction or blessing would then conclude the service.

Since this service will occur in close proximity to Memorial Day, the following lines from the same hymn are appropriate as a prayer response:

> Grant us thy peace throughout our earthly life;
> peace to thy church from error and from strife;
> peace to our land, the fruit of truth and love;
> peace in each heart, thy Spirit from above.

The tune, Ellers, is to be found in most major hymnals, even if these particular sets of words are not.

If Psalm 139 is employed for the entrance and concluding rites, then the Song of Hannah (I Samuel 2:1b-10), discussed above in the Old Testament commentary, may be used as the response to the first lesson or as a canticle or responsive reading in its own right.

The images of Eli's lack of sight, no frequent vision, and the flickering Temple lamp may be related to the image of the light of the knowledge of the glory of God in the epistle lesson. In each case the issue is that of the kind of ministry which is being carried out in God's name in the community. Eli's sons and the super-apostles are not tending the lamp, the treasure that has been entrusted to them. An alternative New Testament lesson, or another reference for illustrative purposes, is Revelation 2:1-7, the message to the Ephesian church, which is threatened with the removal of its lampstand because it has "abandoned the love" it "had at first" (v. 4).

Paul's sobering words that "death is at work in us" may be related to the consequence of Jesus' ministry in today's Gospel, when Jesus' enemies begin to plot his destruction. Paul is not complaining, because he knows that death has been destroyed and that the death of which he speaks will accomplish life for the Corinthians. It is this same trust in the ultimate goodness of God that can account for Eli's resignation to the will of God; even God's word of judgment is a sign that Israel has not been abandoned.

Paul's contention that we do not preach ourselves may provide preachers an opportunity this week to examine how often we use illustrations of personal experience in our sermons, so that at least we pause over the place we play in those anecdotes. Charles Wesley wrote the following commentary on today's Gospel lesson:

> While Jesus lets his followers eat,
>   He suffers hunger still,
> That pastors may themselves forget,
>   And more for others feel:
> By miracle the crowd he fed,
>   Not his own wants supplied,
> He hungered in the people's stead,
>   Thirsted for them, and died!

(S T Kimbrough, Jr. and Oliver A. Beckerlegge, eds., *The Unpublished Poetry of Charles Wesley,* vol. II [Nashville: Kingswood Books, 1990], p. 53)

Proper Five
Sunday Between June 5 and 11
(If After Trinity Sunday)

Old Testament Texts

First Samuel 8 is the story of Israel's request for a king. Psalm 138 is a hymn of thanksgiving by an individual.

The Lesson: *I Samuel 8:4-11 (12-15), 16-20 (11:14-15)*

Living Between the Ideal and the Real

Setting. For additional background on setting see the section on setting from last week, where the simultaneous rising and falling of paired characters in I and II Samuel was described with regard to Samuel and Eli. Many of the issues that were applied to Eli last week come full circle in I Samuel 8 as problems that now plague Samuel. Samuel has continued to rise in power and prestige after his call in I Samuel 3 to the point where he successfully leads Israel in a holy war against the Philistines in I Samuel 7. But his sons, Joel and Abijah, are no good. This fact is mentioned in I Samuel 8:1-3 and is important for interpreting the lesson for this Sunday. It reminds us of Eli, whose sons Hophni and Phinehas were also no good. There is a contrast to be noted in this parallelism, which provides a point of focus for interpretation. Whereas the character flaw in Eli's sons was cultic (sleeping with cultic personnel and eating too much of the sacrifices), the problem with Samuel's sons is ethical (taking bribes and perverting justice). The unethical activity of Samuel's sons introduces the problems of power in general and justice in particular that will be central for the remainder of the chapter.

Structure. As the commentary on setting already implies, I Samuel 8:1-3 is important for the remainder of the chapter and should be included in the lesson for two reasons: (1) it provides the immediate context for the elders' request in vv. 4-6; (2) it prevents a facile, judgmental interpretation of the elders, as if they are sinning by requesting a king. The narrative makes it clear that their request is prompted by the inability of Samuel's sons to carry on the leadership of their father. The text falls into five parts. It begins with the narrator informing the reader that Samuel's sons are incapable of mediating justice in Israel (vv. 1-3). This setting prompts a four-part exchange.

I. The elder's request for a king (vv. 4-6)
II. The divine response (vv. 7-10)
III. Samuel's litany concerning the justice of kings (vv. 11-18)
IV. The people's renewed request for a king (vv. 19-20)

Justice (Hebrew, *mišpat* from the verb *šapat* meaning "to judge") is the central theme of the text, occurring in every section. Three times in the introduction the narrator uses the term *judge* (Hebrew, *šopetim*) or *justice* (Hebrew, *mišpat*), and the message is clear: Samuel's sons perverted justice (v. 3), and although Samuel was himself honest he is not blameless, since he was in fact the one placing them in positions of power as judges (vv. 1-2). The term occurs twice in the speech of the elders, when they request a king "to govern" (Hebrew, *lesaptenu,* literally translates "to judge") them in vv. 5, 6. The divine speech closes in v. 9 with the directive that Samuel show

Israel the "ways of the king" (Hebrew, *mišpat hammelek*, literally "justice of the king"), which is repeated at the outset of Samuel's speech (v. 10 "This will be the ways [Hebrew, *mišpat*] of the king who will reign over you"). Finally the term resurfaces in v. 20 when the people state three reasons why they want a king: to judge them (NRSV "govern"), to go out before them, and to fight for them.

Significance. First Samuel 8 is about power and the just exercise of it in our everyday lives. The text has a practical flavor. It is not about theory, and it does not present a utopian vision of life. Samuel is old, his sons are immoral, and Israel needs leadership. Thus the text makes no claims of presenting an ideal of justice or power that can be embedded in any one character within the story. This is important for preaching this text, because too often it is read simplistically with Samuel being the hero and the elders (and Israel) the anti-heroes. (Such a reading is encouraged by the suggested boundaries of the lectionary text.) When the text is read beginning at v. 4, the elder's request for a king is interpreted as a blatant rejection of the ideal prophet-leader, Samuel, which then marks the transition from the golden age of tribal Israel to the pragmatic age of the kings. Such an interpretation, although neat and clean, is misleading, and in the end it deprives this text of its central message that the practical exercise of power in our everyday communities is always less than ideal and, therefore, must be critically evaluated.

In preaching this story it is important to underscore that there is no hero in this story, nor is there an anti-hero. Instead we are presented with morally ambiguous characters, whose mixed motives are so difficult to unravel that in the end even God seeks a compromise. This problem is reflected in the commentaries, where the determination of motive in characters has remained a problem for scholars. Several points will provide illustration of this. For example, why is Samuel so offended by the request of the elders for a king in vv. 4-6? Is his opposition for religious reasons, namely that a king would challenge Yahweh's lordship over Israel? Or is his opposition political, namely that a king would replace his sons? If we focus on the preceding context (vv. 1-3) and the exact language that the elders use (his sons are unjust), then it would appear that Samuel's opposition is political, in which case we then have the second occurrence in the book of Samuel of how the passing on of power within a family is a problem. If, on the other hand, we focus on the following speech (vv. 7-10), then the conflict appears to be religious, since the kingship of God does become the central issue. It is important to note, however, that it is God who articulates the religious problem of kingship and not Samuel. Determining the motive of the elders is just as difficult. At first their request appears to arise from the moral failure of Samuel's sons, yet their wish to be like "the other nations" raises a red flag, since the people of God are not meant to be like the other nations. Added to the problem of interpreting the motive of the elder's request is that their larger role in Deuteronomistic tradition (those responsible for the writing of Deuteronomy-Kings) is antimonarchical. They are no lovers of kings, yet in our text they are requesting one. Then, finally there is God's "yes, but" answer to the whole situation.

Several points are important for preaching this text. One, justice is inherently theological. Consequently it must be rooted in an ideal vision of what God would have this world be. The ideal of justice for the authors of I Samuel 8 is that there be no earthly king. This ideal is embedded in God's speech in vv. 7-10. Two, regardless of our ideal, the application of justice in complex communities is a far more tentative and provisional matter. The authors of I Samuel 8 underscores this point by not overtly idealizing Samuel, by putting the request for a king in the mouth of characters who would oppose it as an ideal, and by ascribing conditional divine approval to it. Three, because of its provisional nature, the application of justice must be continually and critically evaluated. The closing words in the divine speech to Samuel are: ''Solemnly warn them.'' The urgency of the message in I Samuel 8 for the contemporary church goes without saying. Too many of our moral debates (for example, right to life/pro-choice; sexual orientation) lack the tentativeness that is necessary for the application of justice in complex communities. Ironically and tragically, without this tentativeness, ideals of justice can themselves become unjust.

The Response: *Psalm 138*

A Thanksgiving Hymn

Setting. Psalm 138 is classified as a thanksgiving hymn by an individual. Scholars debate the identity of the individual, which then carries over into a debate about genre and the cultic setting of the hymn. Is the individual a king, making this a royal psalm, or is the singer any member of the community? This debate provides two different ways in which the psalm can be used as a response to I Samuel 8:1-20.

Structure. The psalm separates into three parts. Verses 1-3 are a song of thanksgiving in which the salvation of God is praised in the context of the gods (v. 1*b*). Verses 4-6 shift the focus from the divine realm to the earthly realm of kings. The psalmist underscores how all kings will one day praise God. The psalm ends in vv. 7-8 on a note of confidence. Because God rules in heaven (other gods) and on earth (kings), the psalmist expresses confidence in God's leading through this life.

Significance. The debate about the genre of the hymn (whether it is royal or communal) underscores two ways in which Psalm 138 might be used as a response to I Samuel 8. First, if the royal setting is emphasized, then the psalm provides a positive counterpoint to the negative assessment of the ''justice of kings'' that was outlined by Samuel in I Samuel 8:11-17. In contrast to the exploitative practices of the king that are listed by Samuel, Psalm 138 provides a contrasting perspective on how a king might function when his focus is on

47

God. Second, if the communal setting is emphasized, then the psalm provides an important word of confidence in God's ability to lead even when the application of justice may not be clear. This second use of the psalm is very important, for the danger of tentative decisions about justice is that we give up our ideals altogether for pragmatic solutions. The personal language of trust throughout Psalm 138 provides a safeguard against this danger.

New Testament Texts

Remarkably, in II Corinthians Paul is replying to opponents of his work, and in Mark Jesus comes under fire from critics of his ministry. The issue at the heart of the controversy in both cases is the nature and origin of awesome spiritual power. This theme of divine power as really being God's own power is treated distinctly in our readings, but the texts cohere in their worldview and theology.

The Epistle: *II Corinthians 4:13–5:1*

The What, Why, and How of Christian Service

Setting. We move forward to the next verses of Paul's impassioned discussion of the character of his ministry and the nature of true Christian service, so that it may be profitable to consult the remarks about setting offered in relation to last week's epistle reading. We should recall especially that Paul is under fire at the time of his writing these lines and that he believes there is more at stake than his reputation; indeed, because the apostle regards himself and other believers as servants of the gospel whose lives and patterns of ministry are shaped by the gospel itself, he understands that the truth of the gospel—that is, what is the true gospel—is the point of the controversy.

Structure. The verses of our lesson come in the heart of the larger section, 2:14–7:4. In general, 4:7–5:10 is a discourse on the character and content of valid Christian ministry, which evaluates Christian service in relation to the person and work of Jesus Christ. Here Paul discusses and occasionally declares his confidence despite adversity.

Our text is composed of elements of two larger, coherent units of thought. Verses 13-15 come from 4:7-15, which defines and interprets apostolic ministry as Paul understands it. Then, 4:16–5:1 comes from 4:16–5:5 which declares and explains Paul's confidence or boldness in his style of ministry. The content of these verses is laden with tradition, scripture, and metaphor, so that careful study with the aid of a scholarly commentary is both instructive and suggestive for preaching.

Significance. Paul articulates a sharp contrast between his finite humanity and the infinite power of God. This distinction is necessary to make clear that God is the source of divine power at work in the Christian community. The apostle argues that this is consistent with the paradoxical truth revealed in the Christ event. After launching his explanation of the character of his work (vv. 7-12), Paul extends the argument in vv. 13-15. He begins by quoting Psalm 116:10 exactly (not always his practice!), and he unpacks the citation beyond the clear literal sense of the words to formulate a one-to-one comparison: As the psalmist believed and therefore spoke, so too the apostle believes and therefore speaks. Paul uses the psalm as a scriptural precedent to establish the veracity of his ministry. His point is this: Faith (for Paul, a gift from God that is defined by God) is the foundation of genuine proclamation. This is the "what" of ministry—God-directed faithful proclamation. Then, the apostle expresses his confidence in the character of his work so that he states the content of his message—God who raised Jesus will raise faithful servants with Jesus and in community with other believers. We also learn of the "why"—all valid Christian service is for other believers unto the glory of God.

Paul's reflections further declare and explain his confidence.

He says he is willing to risk his all, despite the reality of adversity, because God sustains him in his labors. Paul's odd references to "inner" and "outer" persons are part of the dualistic anthropological language of his day, but from the context we may paraphrase, "We can spend our life in this world for God because God is already giving us new life that will endure beyond the present even into the context of God's new creation which has already appeared but which is not yet fully present." To illustrate his point Paul sets up a series of contrast between "lessers and greaters." In each of these pairs he points out the inferiority of present existence in comparison to God's promised future, which is already being made real. This reasoning tells us "how" the apostle interpreted the hardships he endured in the course of his ministry and "how" he understood his work to be made possible by God.

The Gospel: *Mark 3:20-35*

Confusion, Conflict, and True Discipleship

Setting. Immediately after telling how Jesus began his ministry in Galilee and called out twelve disciples for special involvement, Mark records a pair of stories that recall the less than positive response of certain persons (family and religious authorities) to Jesus' work. At the outset of the ministry the masses seem favorably inclined toward Jesus, whereas only smaller groups are those with reservations. Through the course of the ministry the pendulum will swing, and we will finally see Jesus abandoned by even his closest associates, but for now the negative reactions of Jesus' family and certain religious authorities is the foreshadowing exception rather than the rule.

Structure. Mark arranges the material in this passage carefully by using a literary technique known as intercalation. Scholars often refer to this style as the Markan "sandwich," meaning that Mark begins a story and, then, tells another before completing the original account. Arranged in this fashion the two stories complement and comment upon each other, achieving more force than the stories could if they were separated or set in tandem.

Here, vv. 20-21 start a story about the concern of the family of Jesus over his behavior. Verses 22-30 break in with the account of a controversy that arose when certain scribes accused Jesus of being a sorcerer in league with the devil ("Beelzebul"). With the conflict story completed, vv. 31-35 return to the family of Jesus and his reaction to their attempt to take charge of him. Thematically the lesson moves from "misunderstanding" to "false accusations and the revelation of God's power" to "defining who truly forms the family of God."

Significance. Jesus' actions and teachings attracted great attention. Perhaps his words and deeds seemed flamboyant and merely generated curiosity, but Mark tells us repeatedly that the multitudes recognized a unique authority in what Jesus said and did. Yet, as the lesson recalls, not all were favorably impressed. At the outset, in the midst of popular acclaim, we find the family of Jesus so concerned about his unusual activities that they assume he is mad; he should be taken home and brought back to his rightful senses. It is striking to find those closest to Jesus among those who do not understand him. Furthermore, their actions, though well intended, are actually in opposition to his purposes in ministry. They want to take charge of him, and they show no awareness that he might be revealing to them the very will of God for their own lives. This story should come as a sobering reminder to persons who take comfort in a close relationship with Jesus that our past associations are not an absolute guarantee of a proper present performance in relation to God's will. We must always be ready to follow in startling new directions as disciples of our Lord, and we must not assume that our past experiences and knowledge mean a correct understanding of new revelations of God's will.

The next group that shows both misunderstanding and hostile resistance to Jesus' ministry is the scribes. These were persons especially well-versed in the law. They were regarded as the authorized, or at least qualified, interpreters of scripture, and thus God's will. Yet when confronted with the amazing work of Jesus Christ, these supposedly sophisticated interpreters were unable to perceive the hand and will of God in that activity. Instead, the scribes concluded that Jesus was in alliance with Satan. Notice they did not deny the reality of the power at work in and through Jesus; their point of contention was not whether there was real power at work, but whose power was active in the ministry of Jesus. Again, we should be shocked and humbled by these events. It is the good religious folks, those who have given a lifetime to study and providing religious leadership who prove to be incapable of comprehending Jesus. Indeed, their learning is a liability, for when Jesus does not fit their set religious expectations they declare that he is the enemy, theirs and God's! The fact is, when we become "at home" in our religious assumptions, when we become convinced we know who God is and what God is about in this world, we are in danger of being incapable of fresh perception of God's new directions in our midst. Sick religion is worse than no religion at all.

In the final scene of the lesson, Jesus clarifies the total situation. Past experiences, associations, and knowledge are not the basis of our relationship to God; rather, we are aligned with God as we respond presently to God's work in the here-and-now. The sense of the lesson has both negative and positive dimensions. We should allow the negative side of the stories to function as humbling reminders that we do not have a relationship with God merely out of our pasts, and we should hear the call of the positive side of the final scene to be open and responsive to God's present work in our lives.

Proper 5: The Celebration

Today's lessons, as the commentary indicates, have running through them a common concern about what it means to be prepared for God's ongoing action in the world and how we need to be ready to encounter change as God's gift. Cardinal Newman said, "To live is to change, and to be perfect is to have changed often." This is not a celebration of change for the sake of change, but a recognition of a process of development, growth, evolution that is at the heart of God's dealing with the universe. It is not the same thing as a doctrine of inevitable progress; rather, it is an affirmation of faith in God's intention for the creation as demonstrated by the radical discontinuity of the cross and Resurrection. The Resurrection was not change accomplished by a committee or team assigned to long-range planning. James Russell Lowell, writing about "The Present Crisis," which for him was the abolitionist movement in the early nineteenth century, clearly understood the ethical dimensions involved in coping with the changes and the accompanying ambiguities brought by the march of time:

> New occasions teach new duties,
> Time makes ancient good uncouth;
> They must upward still and onward,
> Who would keep abreast of truth.

It is easy to parody this as a simple-minded relativism, but more is at work here, and the preacher is called on to help the congregation glimpse the immensity and complexity of the assertion that God's ways are not our ways, and God's thoughts are not our thoughts.

If this approach to the lessons is taken, the following hymn by Charles Wesley would serve well as a hymn of dedication or commitment (tune: St. Catherine or Melita). The third stanza alone can serve as a response to the reading of the Gospel lesson.

> 1. Behold the servant of the Lord!
> I wait thy guiding eye to feel,
> To hear and keep thy every word,
> To prove and do thy perfect will,
> Joyful from my own works to cease,
> Glad to fulfill all righteousness.

2. Me if thy grace vouchsafe to use,
   Meanest of all thy creatures, me,
   The deed, the time, the manner choose;
   Let all my fruit be found of thee;
   Let all my works in thee be wrought,
   By thee to full perfection brought.

3. My every weak though good design
   O'errule or change, as seems thee meet;
   Jesus, let all my work be thine!
   Thy work, O Lord, is all complete,
   And pleasing in thy Father's sight;
   Thou only hast done all things right.

4. Here then to thee thine own I leave;
   Mould as thou wilt thy passive clay;
   But let me all thy stamp receive,
   But let me all thy words obey,
   Serve with a single heart and eye,
   And to thy glory live and die.

Proper Six
Sunday Between June 12
and 18 Inclusive
(If After Trinity Sunday)

Old Testament Texts

First Samuel 15:34–16:13 is the account of the anointing of
David by Samuel. Psalm 20 is a prayer for the king.

The Lesson: *I Samuel 15:34–16:13*

The Risk of Anointing

Setting. The focus of I Samuel changes from Eli and Samuel
to Saul and David in I Samuel 15:34–16:13, with the story of the
anointing of David. An overview of the larger context of
I Samuel will illustrate the important transitional role that this
story plays in the larger account of Saul and David and how
David's anointing puts him on a risk-filled journey. In I Samuel
8, Saul is anointed to be the first leader of Israel and for eight
chapters the reader follows his rise in power until I Samuel 15,
which marks his downfall, and prepares the reader for the rise of
David. First Samuel 16 begins with a motif of mourning when
God asks Samuel how long he will lament the fall of Saul. The
implied answer to the question is that he should not be mourning
Saul at all, because there is a new king that must be anointed.
The command for Samuel to "fill his horn with oil" introduces

the central motif of our Old Testament lesson, since the goal of this story is for Samuel to discover and to anoint this new king. With the anointing of David, I Samuel becomes a story of his rise and Saul's decline. (Note the contrast between I Samuel 16:13 and v. 14 about how the Spirit of God simultaneously descends on David and departs from Saul.) As any reader of I Samuel knows, however, the rise of David is risk-filled. He is anointed into a whirlwind of threats by a giant, by Saul, by enemy nations, and so on, his only security is the promise of God's protection.

Structure. First Samuel 15:34–16:13 separates into three parts, each of which includes a divine speech to Samuel and an account of Samuel's obedient response. The text can be outlined in the following manner:

I. The Command to Anoint a New King (15:34–16:5)
   A. The first divine command and response by Samuel (15:34–16:3) (The risk of anointing of new king)
   B. The obedience of Samuel (vv. 4-5)
II. The Search for a New King (vv. 6-11)
   A. Samuel's choice and the second divine command (vv. 6-7) (The problem of perception)
   B. The obedience of Samuel (vv. 8-11)
III. The Anointing (vv. 12-13)
   A. The third divine command (v. 12)
   B. The obedience of Samuel (v. 13)

Significance. Even though the central theme of this text is about the anointing of David, nevertheless, the outline underscores how Samuel (rather than David) is really the central character within the story itself. Thus Samuel deserves our attention in exploring the importance of anointing, because in many ways his role within the story illustrates many of the risk-filled aspects of David's anointing that will be played out in the larger structure of I Samuel.

The risks to Samuel in anointing David are stated clearly in his first response to God in v. 2: "How can I go? If Saul hears it, he will kill me." God's response to Samuel is that he must take a heifer for sacrificing (supposedly as a ruse to Saul) and that God would then point out the future king during the sacrifice. The first scene closes with the narrator underscoring Samuel's faithfulness. Yet God's closing promise that he would make known to Samuel which one of Jesse's sons must be anointed as the new king provides the stage for Samuel's next problem, namely how to choose. Samuel immediately picks Eliab (presumably because he is the most striking in appearance), prompting the divine caution that God's anointing is not in response to outward appearance. Instead "the Lord looks on the heart." Once again Samuel is obedient to God's directions, and thus he continues the search through all of Jesse's sons. The final scene opens with the divine command in v. 12 that Samuel anoint the child David, which Samuel does in v. 13 prompting an unleashing of the Spirit of God.

In using this text, the preacher may want to underscore that there are obstacles both in being anointed by God and in trying to carry out God's command to anoint. David embodies the former and Samuel the latter. The obstacles, however, are very similar for both characters. There is risk because the power of God's anointing frequently is at odds with our notions of power. David will learn this lesson successfully in confronting the giant Goliath and then fail at it when he exploits the power to rule in the affair with Bathsheba (II Samuel 11). Samuel is successful in our lesson only because he learns to follow God even against his own best judgments.

The Response: *Psalm 20*

A Prayer for the King

Setting. Psalm 20 is a prayer for the king. Note the reference to the Lord's anointed in v. 5. There is a clear liturgical progression to the psalm from petitions addressed to the king in vv. 1-5 (note the use of *you*) to a response by the king in vv. 6-8 (note the use of *I*). Scholars debate the specific occasion that might have given rise to such a liturgy (for example, a New Year Festival or an Enthronement Festival). The imagery in vv. 7-8 of chariots and horses suggest that it may have been a prayer for the king used prior to war.

Structure. The liturgical structure provides a clear outline in three parts: the petitions for the king (vv. 1-5), the response by the king (vv. 6-8), and a concluding petition (v. 9).

Significance. Psalm 20 provides a fitting complement to I Samuel 15:34–16:13 because it is an elaboration of what the special power of being God's anointed means. Two aspects of power stand out in the psalm: divine protection and special access to God in prayer. First, protection: Central to the psalm is the power of the divine name to protect the king. The name of God is called upon for protection in v. 1*b* and acknowledged as the source of victory in v. 5*a*. This protection is then recognized by the king in v. 7*b* as a source of pride. Second, special access to God in prayer: Twice in the opening section of the psalm petition is made for the king to have special access to God (vv. 4, 5*b*). The opening response of the king in v. 6, "Now I know that the LORD will help his anointed" then provides illustration of the king's special relationship with God both through his recognition of divine help and through his claiming the title, "anointed." The psalm moves from king to community in the closing line, where both the motifs of protection ("Give victory to the king, O LORD") and special access to God through prayer ("Answer us when we call") are placed in the larger context of the worshiping community.

New Testament Texts

The lessons lead us in quite different directions in our reflection, although both express major themes of Christian thinking. In distinct ways both texts articulate an eschatological perspective; both texts declare the promise, hope, and reality of divine transformation of human existence in the context of the redemption of creation; and both texts register the inadequacy and impossibility of evaluating God's redemptive work in terms of this world's standards.

The Epistle: *II Corinthians 5:6-10 (11-13), 14-17*

Christian Confidence Through Transformation in Christ

Setting. Readers are asked to consult the discussion of setting and structure for the epistle lesson for Proper 5 before considering the following comments. This week's lesson is part of Paul's conclusion to the line of argumentation and reasoning over the past three to four chapters. The concern is the character and content of Christian ministry in relation to the reality of the crucified and raised Lord Jesus Christ.

Structure. The verses of the lesson come from two subsections that commentators usually distinguish from each other: 4:7–5:10, the first part of which we encountered last week, and 5:11-19, which builds off the previous section and seeks to summarize the entire reflection from 2:14 to this point immediately prior to the full blown appeal Paul will make in 6:1–7:4. (It may prove beneficial to include vv. 18-19 or 18-21 in the reading of the lesson.) Thus, we may think of the verses of the lesson as falling into two parts with distinct themes and moods: (1) a highly declarative statement of Christian confidence that calls believers toward the future and (2) a profound theological statement about the marvelous transformation of human life through the reconciling power of God at work in Jesus Christ.

Significance. The lesson begins with another affirmation of the confidence of the apostle about the legitimacy of his mission and message. In part, vv. 6-10 reformulate the idea of boldness declared in 4:16*a*. The key to this portion of the lesson is the way in which v. 10 casts Paul's whole line of reasoning in an eschatological frame of judgment, meaning Christian accountability. (The same basic idea is articulated in I Corinthians 3:10-15.) Unfortunately, out of context these verses can look very mercenary, as if the apostle lived and advised other Christians to live according to a simple reward and retribution scheme. But, coming on the heels of 4:16–5:5 these verses attempt to orient the thinking of the readers away from a mere concern with the present and toward God's future so that all present behavior of believers is determined in relation to, or even as a result of, God's future.

From this call to concern with and investment of our lives in God's future Paul moves to speak of the "fear of the Lord," a well-known notion from the Old Testament denoting appropriate reverence toward God and attendant manners of life. Verses 11-13 have a polemical undertone and are most likely related to those in Corinth whom Paul is opposing (the "super-apostles")—namely, "those who are boasting of what is outward and not what is inward." The test of valid Christian living (and ministry) is whether or not it is directed toward God and toward others—no matter its superficial appearance—rather than toward the self. As Paul puts the matter in v. 14, believers live faithful lives because Christ's own love grips them, freeing them from a preoccupation with self and freeing them for a thorough relation with Christ.

Verses 16-17 (or, perhaps better 16-19 or 16-21) ponder the wonderful truth of the transformation of human life through the believers' association with Christ. The conceptual content of these verses is overwhelming. The change of life that results from our affiliation with Christ means that we no longer relate to

Christ or to others according to the normal standards of this world. Paul's vision moves to a cosmic perspective in relation to creation and God's new creation being brought forth in and through God's work in Jesus Christ. At the heart of Paul's eschatology, seen here as it was in v. 10, we find an "already/not yet" pattern of contrasting and speaking about this world and God's promise of a fully redeemed creation. Paul understands that while God's work in Jesus Christ means that "already" the advent of the new creation is occurring, still God's new order is "not yet" fully present; but while it may "not yet" be fully realized, "already" for those who believe the new creation has dawned in their lives which are the evidence of the beginning of God's realization of God's promises. We do not merely await the promise of God's reconciling redemptive work, because in Jesus Christ and in the lives of those who believe in him we see the reality of reconciling redemption.

The Gospel: *Mark 4:26-34*

The Inscrutable Character of God's Saving Ways

Setting. In the gospel according to Mark we regularly find materials clustered together because of similar literary types and themes. Mark 13 collects teachings about the future. Portions of Mark 6–8 and 4–6 preserve cycles of miracle stories. The same phenomenon seems to occur in Mark 4:1-34 where we find a series of parables uttered by Jesus. Our lesson comes from the ending of the parables cluster and includes both parables and Mark's explanatory report about the purpose of Jesus' teaching in parabolic speech.

Structure. Broadly viewed our passage falls into three parts. Verses 26-29 record teaching usually referred to as the parable of the seed growing secretly (or mysteriously); vv. 30-32 recount the parable of the mustard seed; and vv. 33-34 offer Mark's remarks about Jesus' parables. In preaching one may focus on either parable alone, or either of the parables in conjunction with the remarks in vv. 33-34, or the entire lesson; although it would be practically impossible to deal with the details of the whole lesson without becoming protracted and repetitive.

Significance. The central concern of both parables is indicated in the declaration of v. 26 and the questions of v. 30—namely, the kingdom of God. Before moving into further consideration of these parables and Mark's final statement, however, we should take note of an ongoing debate among scholars about the exact meaning of the phrase most often translated "kingdom of God." Many interpreters insist that we miss the primary sense of the phrase when we think in geographical or local terms rather than in the dynamic sense of "reign," which the Greek word *basileia* carries along with "kingdom." Emphasizing this dynamic quality of God's lordship helps us think about and recognize the current character of God's work in this world. We are not misled into simply looking for some wholly (and, holy!) other place that implies God is not at work in the context of the present world. Yet, as helpful as this line of interpretation is, not emphasizing the spatial dimension of the kingdom of God can mislead us into misreading the topic of these parables in terms of a fully realized eschatology—or, put another way, in terms of a potentially realizable reality in this world. To read the text in this fashion is to take a mistaken step backwards toward the vision of genuine nineteenth-century liberalism with its somewhat Pelagian emphasis on human achievement; whereas to maintain a clear concept of God's space is a reminder that the coming of the kingdom is a gracious divine accomplishment. The genuine difficulty of speaking directly about the kingdom of God registers in Jesus' own searching words of introduction to each parable in the lesson.

What is the point of the comparison in the first parable? Is the kingdom like the mysteriously growing seed? Or the peculiar farmer? Or the land? Or all these elements? One is sorely tempted to turn this intriguing parable into an allegory by identifying each of the story elements with someone or something, but as scholars who work regularly with parables point out, such reduction of dynamics forces singularity of meaning from a story form that moves creatively beyond narrow communication. This parable confronts us with the story of mysterious events that elude banal comprehension. The kingdom of God is happening, and for those who are attentive there are clear signs of its reality. But we do not control the wonderful work of God, although we are caught up in it and it has meaning for our lives. Above all, the conclusion of the parable tells us that the mysterious kingdom of God calls us toward God's goals and places a stringent, urgent demand upon us for appropriate action in relation to what God is accomplishing and calling us to do.

The second parable is equally enticing and difficult. In the first place the mustard seed is not the smallest seed on the earth, although it was regarded as such by ancient Jews and referred to as such in other places. Yet Jesus' parable is not a botany lesson, nor is it a moral lesson. The parable speaks of the kingdom. Perhaps we are to think of the contrast between the seemingly small seed and the sizable shrub that grows from it. But even here the images of the parable are striking. The mustard shrub is surely no cedar of Lebanon, no giant sequoia, no live oak, no California redwood. What God is doing is not according to human standards and expectations; but it is still what God is doing. God's work accomplishes benefits, though they are clearly God's designs and not the plans of humans. Can we see God's hand where we might not be looking for it? Can we affirm, appreciate, and be grateful for God's work and goodness, although God's ends may present us with outcomes different from those we desire, design, and demand? It may be hard for us to hear of the kingdom since what God is doing is seemingly other than what we would likely do if we were God. But Jesus' words call for us to listen.

Proper 6: The Celebration

Professor Soards's comment on the epistle and Gospel lessons that they "register the inadequacy and impossibility of evaluating God's redemptive work in terms of this world's standards" applies equally well to the Old Testament lesson with its message that mortals "look on the outward appearance, but the Lord looks on the heart." The anointing of David could be illustrative for a sermon based on either of the New Testament texts.

Christian liturgy has long understood the anointing of kings in the Old Testament to be a way of helping Christians understand the meaning of their baptism, when they become part of a "royal priesthood." Anointing with oil is a part of some baptismal rites. Seen from this sacramental perspective, the text may be used to discuss how much more important divine election is than human conventional wisdom. It may also help people affirm their importance in God's sight, regardless of the estimation in which they hold themselves or are held by others. If Psalm 20 is used, it should be made clear in this instance that the congregation is referring to itself when it says that "the Lord will help his anointed." There is also a christological interpretation that may be given to the psalm, so that we are anointed only to the degree that we are in Christ through baptism, for it is he who is the Anointed One (Christ = Anointed One). Obviously an appropriate opening hymn for today is "Hail to the Lord's Anointed."

The reference to the new creature in the epistle lesson suggests the use of "Love Divine, All Loves Excelling," with its line, "Finish then thy new creation." This would be an appropriate closing hymn particularly if the sermon dealt with baptism as a process rather than a static event.

A fitting response to the Gospel lesson is the second stanza of "Come, Ye Thankful People Come," beginning "All the world is God's own field" (except in *The Baptist Hymnal* [1991], which has "We ourselves are God's own field").

Proper Seven
Sunday Between June 19 and 25 Inclusive
(If After Trinity Sunday)

Old Testament Texts

First Samuel 17 is the account of how David killed the giant Goliath. Psalm 9 is a hymn of praise.

The Lesson: *I Samuel 17:(1a, 4-11, 19-23) 32-49*

Charismatic Leadership

Setting. The books of the Old Testament are made up of smaller, once independent stories that are now stitched together to form larger narratives. Redactors (those responsible for the editing and present arrangement of the material) have brought together two stories about David's extraordinary powers in I Samuel 16–17 (his ability to ward off evil spirits by playing music and his ability to kill giants). The present formation of these stories is intriguing because the redactors have departed from strict chronology and from narrative logic to tell us these stories. Note, for example, how in I Samuel 16:18-23 David is introduced to Saul as a musician, a warrior, and a man of valor, and how he joins Saul's entourage so that he can continue to ward off evil spirits through his gift of musical muse. Yet in chapter 17, when Saul is confronting Goliath and the rest of the

Philistine army, David must be introduced anew to Saul as a small shepherd boy (see here especially I Samuel 17:58). Then note how the giant Philistine warrior is named Goliath only twice (vv. 4, 23), as compared to the more frequent reference simply to "the Philistine" (for example, v. 10). This in itself might only be a stylistic device of the writer. On the other hand, it may indicate that the story of David's defeat of the giant has itself gone through stages of development from an unnamed giant to Goliath. The latter suggestion acquires force when we note that in II Samuel 21:19 a warrior, Elhanan son of Jaareorigim, is also attributed with killing a giant named Goliath, "the shaft of whose spear was like a weavers beam" (see I Samuel 17:7). Too often an analysis of tradition history and redaction (as we have done here) is viewed suspiciously as an attempt to undermine the authority of a text. This is unfortunate because these tools of exegesis can actually aid us in focusing on proper questions for interpretation. By bringing together two distinct traditions of David's early rise to power without harmonizing them into a continuous story, and by freely incorporating motifs from other characters, redactors force us to look for some criteria other than chronology, narrative logic, or historicity to uncover the purpose of the stories. We have in I Samuel 16–17 two distinct traditions that are held together by the common theme of David's charismatic power of leadership, as evidenced in music and in war. The quality of such leadership will be the focus for interpretation.

Structure. I Samuel 17 presents a problem because of its size. The lectionary committee has sought to address this problem by recommending vv. 1b (the setting of war with the Philistines), vv. 4-11 (the introduction of Goliath, his massive size and his challenge), and vv. 19-23 (the arrival of David to the battleground). You may wish to adjust this reading in light of your own study of the chapter. The lectionary text focuses on vv. 32-49, which separates into four parts:

I. David's Request to Fight the Giant (vv. 32-37)
II. David's Preparation for Battle (vv. 38-40)
III. The Exchange Between David and the Giant (vv. 41-47)
IV. David Kills the Giant (vv. 48-49)

The chapter concludes by describing how Israel routed the Philistines after David killed the giant.

Significance. The primary aims of I Samuel 16–17 are to make David into a legitimate charismatic leader and to provide guidelines for the reader on how to evaluate the nature of charismatic leadership. The first aim, the authority of David, is easy to see and requires little comment. David has extraordinary powers that appear to spring from his character, thus, making him a worthy candidate for king. This story, however, is about more than David. It is also meant to provide guidelines on how we evaluate charismatic leadership, and it is this second aim that provides a springboard for preaching.

Charisma is defined as an "extraordinary power" or as "a personal magic of leadership arousing special popular loyalty." Several aspects of I Samuel 17 build on this definition, while also providing more detailed guidelines for recognizing charismatic leadership in our communities. First, charismatic qualities tend not to be inherited. Instead, they spring up like gifts in an individual as special signs of the Spirit of God. Note how David's brother Eliab shares none of David's traits (vv. 28-30). Second, charismatic qualities are extraordinary. In order to emphasize this point in I Samuel 17, David's natural abilities are played down through a series of contrasts: a giant versus a boy (vv. 33, 41-42), the massive armor of the giant versus David's inabilities to wear any (vv. 4-6, 38-39), the enormous weapons of the giant versus David's slingshot (vv. 7, 40). Third, the motivation of a charismatic leader should not be self-interested but always religiously rooted, which then is also the source of the charismatic power. Pure motivation is the greatest struggle for the gifted charismatic leader. Two contrasts underscore this point: (1) the Israelite soldiers talk of wealth for the one who would kill the giant in contrast to David's religious motivation to kill the giant because he defies God (vv. 24-27, 36-37, 45-47), (2) the fear of Saul and the Israelite army versus David's lack of fear and predication that God would kill the giant (vv. 11, 24, 46). Fourth, charismatic leadership is never seized or assumed. Rather it is always clearly recognized by the larger community, and only on the basis of this recognition is leadership granted. Everyone sees David kill the giant. And, fifth, charismatic leadership functions in service to the larger community. It ceases to be charismatic if it becomes self-interested. After David kills the giant, Israel is able to rout the Philistines. Furthermore, David doesn't end the story by being king.

I Samuel 17 prompts two kinds of reflection for preaching. On the one hand it encourages spontaneous charismatic leadership where it is clearly visible. Frequently leadership becomes inherited and predictable in churches. I Samuel 17 is a challenge to such predictable and controlled communities. On the other hand, the concept of charismatic leadership is on the rise in some sections of the contemporary church. Yet all too often it functions in a highly individualistic context, making such leadership vulnerable to self-interest. The story of David the giant killer provides a series of guidelines for evaluating the charismatic leadership of both lay persons and clergy in such communities.

The Response: *Psalm 9:9-20*

A Hymn of Praise

Setting. Psalm 9 and 10 form a single unit. Several factors lead to this conclusion. The Greek translation (Septuagint) lists both psalms as one and, even though the Hebrew Bible (Masoretic Text) numbers the psalms separately, it includes a division marker between the two psalms, which normally only occurs between strophes within psalms. Also when the two psalms are read together they form an acrostic, with each strophe beginning with a different letter of the Hebrew alphabet. Two conclusions concerning the form of Psalm 9 follow: (1) it probably is not a complete psalm by itself, and (2) there is no alternative structure other than the divisions that are determined by the acrostic pattern.

Structure. Because the lectionary committee is sensitive to how long a congregation will patiently listen to the reading of a doxological hymn, they have abbreviated the selection to twelve verses. In preaching the psalm one can select any number of themes that are driven by the alphabet. The following structure emerges with the Hebrew alphabet: (*alef*) vv. 1-2, intention to praise, (*bet*) vv. 3-4, reasons for confidence; (*gimel*) vv. 5-6, reflection on divine deliverance; (*dalet*) absent; (*he*) vv. 7-8, confession of divine rule and judgeship over the nations; (*waw*) vv. 9-10, divine refuge for the oppressed; (*zayin*) vv. 11-12, a call to praise; (*het*) vv. 13-14, prayer for deliverance; (*tet*) vv. 15-16, inevitable judgment on the nations; (*yod*) v. 17, the end result of the nations; (*kaf*) vv. 18-20, reasons for confidence and a call for deliverance.

Significance. Psalm 9 obviously covers a wide range of themes in a variety of speech forms. The interrelated themes of God's judgment on the nations and salvation for Israel finds a counterpart in the confrontation between David and Goliath. Perhaps the psalm might best be used as a liturgy within the worship service, for example, as a congregational response to the narrative about David and Goliath.

New Testament Texts

As an analogy to the narratives about charismatic power in the actions of David, these lessons draw our attention to the meaning of the power of God at work in Jesus Christ. Paul writes of God's power to the Corinthians to inform them of its character, its meaning, and its implications for their lives.

Mark's narrative tells of the power of God at work in Jesus. The story bears witness to the surprising revelation of that power and its declaration of the all-encompassing nature of God's might.

The Epistle: *II Corinthians 6:1-13*

God's Time, God's Power, and Our Lives

Setting. Once again readers are asked to consult the discussion of setting and structure for the epistle lesson for Proper 5. Our lesson takes us into the last sections of Paul's defense of his style of ministry and brings us to the point that the apostle makes a strong pastoral appeal to the Corinthians.

Structure. There are three identifiable movements in Paul's thinking in these verses. First, in vv. 1-2 the foregoing statements about reconciliation and the role that Christians play in God's work are extended by identifying the crucial moment in which the apostle and the Corinthians live. Then, vv. 3-10 support Paul's appeal to the Corinthians by relating something of the apostle's credentials to the readers. Finally, vv. 11-13 move in a new direction by issuing a pastoral appeal, although this plea follows the previous words of explanation. Commentators frequently point out how neatly 6:11-13 and 7:2-4 fit together, so that one preparing to preach on the epistle may do well to notice the parallel verses in the subsequent chapter. The flow of themes may be suggestive for forming the sermon. The lesson moves from (1) when we live (in a Christ-determined time) to (2) how we live (in a Christ-like manner) to (3) what that means in relation to others (mutual Christian affection and vulnerability).

Significance. In 5:18-19 Paul sketched out a pattern which summarizes his view of reality. He makes this outline emphatic by repeating it twice, back-to-back:

First, 18*a* All this is from God
  18*b* who reconciled us to himself through Christ
  18*c* and has given us the ministry of reconciliation;

Second, that is,

19a God was
19b in Christ reconciling the world to himself
19c^1 not counting their trespasses against them
19c^2 and entrusting the message of reconciliation to us.

Here, God is the source of reconciliation, Christ is the means of reconciliation, and reconciliation means ministry for believers. We see that Paul's thinking about God's work in and through Christ eventuates in reflection about the meaning of that divine work for a life of Christian ministry by believers. With his focus set on the substance and shape of faithful Christian life, Paul moves in the initial verses of this week's lesson to declare that God's future is now setting the course of the present for believers. Taking Isaiah 49:8 as his text, Paul presents his case that now is the time of God's salvation. Thus Paul identifies the time in eschatological terms, which demand full attention and commitment from the Corinthians. The point is plain: God has acted in such a manner that life is no longer the same, rather it has been redefined and reoriented by what God has done and is doing in Jesus Christ—particularly through the faithful ministry of members of the Christian community.

With this perspective clearly established, Paul supports his appeal to the Corinthians by relating his credentials to them. The aim of the argument is to establish that Paul does what God would have him to do and as God would have him do it. The rhetoric in vv. 4-10 is grand in form, and it is possible for contemporary readers to become lost in Paul's description of his ministry so that they miss his point. In essence, the rhetorical scheme supports two related contentions: First, the Holy Spirit is the means of the apostle's ministry (and, for that matter, of all believers' ministry); and second, the power for Christian ministry comes from God. Throughout the argument Paul presents an ironic truth as he examines the appearance of his ministry from two radically different points of view. From the perspective of the present age, to purely human eyes, Paul appears pathetic or even despicable; yet, from the perspective of the new creation, to God's own eyes (and to new eyes given by God), Paul possesses everything and is faultless, steadfast, pure, knowledgeable, patient, kind, holy, genuine, and so on—all because he is sustained through adversity by God.

Finally, Paul turns more directly to the Corinthians and begins to make an appeal to them that they may be as open, honest, and vulnerable in relation to him as he has been to them. Mutual Christ-like care and concern is the apostle's goal. He lays himself open to the Corinthians, and he asks them to reciprocate.

From the logic of 5:18-19 the unnamed model of such unobstructed relating is, of course, Christ himself who is the means of God's salvation. In turn, the source of believers' ability to relate to one another in openness, honesty, and generosity is none other than God.

The Gospel: *Mark 4:35-41*

"Who Then Is This?"

Setting. Following the section on parables Mark's Gospel moves to recount a series of miracle stories that scholars conclude belonged to a very old (before Mark's writing) collection of stories about awesome deeds done by Jesus. The verses of our lesson are loosely related to the foregoing events, but for all practical purposes they begin a section of the account that finds meaning in the overall context of Mark's Gospel but that could occur elsewhere in the entire narrative with little effect on the whole.

Structure. In form this story is like a standard Hellenistic miracle story. First, there is a problem. Then, the miracle worker takes some action in relation to the difficulty. Finally, there is a resolution of the matter, which is accompanied by some clear confirmation from observers. The vocabulary used in this story points beyond a mere "nature miracle" and recalls the acts of God in creation when chaos was overcome and order was brought as God effected the creation of the land, living creatures, and so on. Though the form of the story fits that of standard miracle accounts, the language points toward greater conclusions than merely that Jesus did something dramatic and mind-boggling. The words of the story themselves fill out the structure with the claim that, here, in the activity of Jesus we see the very creative power of God at work in the world for the benefit of those associated with Jesus.

Significance. The story presents Jesus as the master of the sea, a vital theme in the mind of Israel. Water was thought to be the domain of demons, and the sea itself was under the sway of Leviathan, or even Satan, and so in diametric opposition to God. The Israelites feared the sea. As a nation they ventured into marine activity with great hesitation, preferring to stay on dry land in the security of God's power (which was not, in their minds, clearly dominant over the sea!). Israel was not a seafaring people, and in their minds God was at war with the wild forces that ruled the sea.

Already to this point in Mark's narrative we have witnessed Jesus' power in teaching, confirmed by his defeat of the demonic forces that plague human existence and hamper people from the life that God intends for them. But thus far, the battle between Jesus and the forces of evil has taken place on dry ground. Now, however, the scene shifts as Jesus and his followers venture onto the perilous waves of the sea where they are driven by fierce and threatening winds. Jesus has power, but how much? Who exactly is this "son of God" at work in the world in opposition to the real forces of evil? At the end of this story Jesus' own disciples are left asking such a question. But Mark narrates these events so that the readers see more than the disciples who were actually there in the boat. While the disciples are left asking, "Who then is this?" any astute reader of Scripture sees in the activity of Jesus the power of God at work overcoming the perils of chaos that threatened the existence of the characters in this story.

The contrast between the behavior and attitude of the disciples on the one hand and the actions and demeanor of Jesus on the other are telling. Jesus sleeps through the storm. It is not that he is unconcerned with the reality of evil or that he is uncaring about the fate of his disciples, but he is not overcome with anxiety, as they are, because he alone demonstrates full confidence in the presence and the power of God to deal with the threats of the sea. He alone is the one with sufficient faith—perhaps he alone is the one with any faith—to allow him to leave matters in the caring and powerful hands of God, who can and will save. Being tossed about on the sea is not a cause of concern for Jesus, for he knows that God is present and able to calm the storm. Moreover, as he speaks and the elements of nature obey, we see clearly that Jesus is the one in and through whom the saving power of God is at work in the world for the well-being of humanity.

Preachers commonly "spiritualize" this story, using its elements and angles to form lessons about God's work in relation to the human spirit—for example, "Christ stills the storms of our souls," or "faith in Christ brings peace amidst perils." These translations of Mark's account can unintentionally lead those hearing the sermons to conclude that God through Christ cannot really accomplish anything in this crass physical world except to sooth a few spirits—not exactly Mark's point. Better use of this passage might tell of God's real work in the midst of real problems—wars, crimes, drugs, or even natural catastrophes—for the benefit of struggling humankind. Yet, here we should not lose sight of two things: (1) God's work through Jesus, which today repeats itself through the efforts of God-empowered humans, intervenes in crises and alters the course of events; and (2) Jesus Christ is the one through whom the power of God is still at work in the world overcoming the reality of evil.

Proper 7: The Celebration

The division of verses in today's Old Testament lesson will make a smooth reading difficult unless the reader is very well acquainted with the text. If all the verses listed are to be used, it would be helpful to type out a manuscript for reading that flows together and omits the verses excluded by the lectionary. For effective reading, the typeface should be large and the text should be rendered in sense or breath lines. *The Lectionary Bible* (Abingdon Press, 1992) is a helpful resource in these regards.

The dramatic development of 1 Samuel 17 makes one regret the necessity of having to abbreviate it for public reading at all. Pastors and worship committees might wish seriously to discuss whether it would be better to omit one or, unless the Eucharist is being celebrated, even both of the other lessons in order to give the time needed for an effective reading of the entire chapter. This presumes that the reading will be done in a way that conveys the power and dramatic movement of the narrative.

When St. Bernard preached on this story to the monks of Clairvaux, he allegorized Goliath as the sin of pride and the five smooth stones David chose from the brook as the words of Scripture that we use to fight against pride: the word of warning, the word of promise, the word of charity, the word of example, and the word of prayer. He concluded the sermon by describing what it means to slay Goliath with Goliath's own sword:

> Cut off his head with his own sword, destroying vanity by means of the very vanity wherewith you have been attacked. For if you make the feeling of elation that stirs within your mind a motive and a reason for greater humility, condemning yourselves as proud men, and becoming thereafter more humble and abject in your conceit of yourselves, then in truth Goliath has been slain with the sword of Goliath. (*St. Bernard's Sermons for the*

Seasons and Principal Feasts of the Year [Westminster, Md.: Carroll Press, 1950], p. 323)

The theme of the power of God is common to all the lessons today. How the preacher deals with the theme will depend upon which text is taken as primary for the sermon, since the lessons taken together deal with much more than one sermon could encompass.

"Thou Hidden Source of Calm Repose" is appropriate to the theme. It is a little known Wesley text, appearing in *The United Methodist Hymnal* (no. 153), but, during these summer days with the choir perhaps on vacation, it can be used as a solo response between the last two lessons.

Proper Eight
Sunday Between June 26
and July 2 Inclusive

Old Testament Texts

Second Samuel 1 is David's lament for Saul and Jonathan. Psalm 130 is a psalm of hope.

The Lesson: *II Samuel 1:1, 17-27*

Finding Words for Tragedy

Setting. Redactors have taken a funeral dirge from the book of Jashar, entitled "Song of the Bow," and woven it into the larger story of David so that it is now presented as his lament. These kinds of editorial insertions create problems for interpretation in the present context because, even though the subject matter of the dirge is clearly Saul and Jonathan, David, as the singer, now overshadows the psalm. Is the dirge meant to be commentary on the tragic characters Saul and Jonathan? Or is it meant to explore the sorrow of David? These choices, of course, are not either-or decisions, but they do imply somewhat different perspectives for preaching. Most commentaries interpret the song from the perspective of David and thus use the language to explore his sorrow for Saul and especially for Jonathan. Another avenue for preaching is to explore the dirge

77

as concluding commentary on the previous narratives of Saul and Jonathan. From this point of view the psalm gives articulation to unexplainable tragedy that is embedded in the characters of Saul and Jonathan.

Structure. The lectionary text divides between narrative introduction and title (vv. 1, 17-18) and the song (vv. 19-27). The song is a dirge or funerary lament. With regard to form, such songs are composed in kinah meter, which is unbalanced 3 + 2 meter (the word is used in v. 17 to describe the song). Thus the very sound of the poetry carries mood for the hearer, as, for example, minor key music might suggest in contemporary society. Dirges are also frequently introduced with the Hebrew exclamation "How!" (*'ek*), as is the case in the recurring refrain in II Samuel 1:19, 25, 27 ("How the mighty have fallen!"). With regard to content, dirges are eulogies for the dead that are specific in their imagery. Thus they refer to the actual event of death, depict the situation, and address the dead directly in second person, without mentioning God. An exact structure to the dirge in vv. 19-27 is difficult to determine. Two strophes of unequal length are suggested by the content and refrains: Verses 19-25 express mourning the loss of Saul and Jonathan and this section is framed by refrains in vv. 19, 25*a*. Verses 25*b*-27 are words of lament for Jonathan, which conclude with the refrain.

Significance. The dirge provides commentary on the tragic characters Saul and Jonathan. A quick overview of the character development of primarily Saul, but also Jonathan, brings to light a certain uneasiness in how their stories develop. Saul is introduced as tall and strong and certainly not out for personal power. While Saul was looking for his father's donkeys, God chooses him to be king (I Samuel 9). His inherent charismatic power is confirmed in the following chapter when the "spirit of God possessed him," prompting him to prophesy (I Samuel 10:9-13). Saul immediately takes up his task as a holy warrior by defeating the Ammonites (I Samuel 11), but then he falls in disfavor, for what might arguably be as much Samuel's fault as his own. After waiting seven days for a tardy Samuel to arrive at Gilgal in order to perform sacrifice for holy war against the Philistines, Saul took the responsibility on himself, prompting a curse from Samuel (once he got there) and the prediction of the downfall of his house (I Samuel 13). This is the beginning of the end for Saul. Even though he continues in his role as a holy warrior, he makes mistakes. In what appears to be an attempt to compensate for his intrusion into the cult in the previous chapter, Saul makes a pious, but rash oath in I Samuel 14, and, then, to make matters worse, he spares a king's life in I Samuel 15A, prompting Samuel's anger and God's rejection. Divine rejection is so strong that Saul's heartfelt confession of guilt and killing of the king seems not to matter at all (I Samuel 15B), for the next thing we learn is that one of God's evil spirits is set loose to torment him (I Samuel 16:17), while behind the scenes, and unbeknownst to Saul, a new king is already chosen. At this point it becomes clear that Saul is destined for his suicidal death, but not before he sinks into insanity.

Saul is a tragic character because his fate is far worse than his actions. Does he really deserve divine indifference and then divine hostility? Whatever happened to divine forgiveness? There is an uneasiness in the story of Saul, because he is more a victim of divine sovereignty than an active opponent of it, and his story appears to have been constructed to underscore this point. He is a character caught in a web of God's choosing rather than his own, and the only apparent point in the story where he has any control after this is in his suicide. In all of this Jonathan looms in the background as an even more innocent victim, who is destined to go down with the ship.

There is much material here for preaching, but the topic is certainly not an easy one. Sometimes the course of events in a life are not explainable in neat theological systems. For the writers of I and II Samuel, Saul represents such a person. Their dirge for Saul and Jonathan is meant to give voice to this kind of situation. There are no theological explanations in the dirge, simply grief that builds through the repetition of the refrains: "How the mighty have fallen!" "How the mighty have fallen in battle!" "How the mighty have fallen and the weapons of war perished!"

The Response: *Psalm 130*

A Soliloquy on Community

Setting. The penitential prayer of Psalm 130 provides the liturgical language of how we petition for God's grace when we become aware of our shame. This is a powerful psalm. The setting of the psalm is ambiguous. Yet two things are clear. First, the psalmist is at a great distance from God. And, second, the speaker is painfully self-conscious of just how alienated he or she is from God. Thus there is a desperate quality to the opening petitions.

Structure. Psalm 130 separates into four parts. Verses 1-3 move quickly through a cry for help (vv. 1-2), a confession of sin (v. 3), and the realization of grace in God (v. 4). The remainder of the psalm moves out of the insight of v. 4 and begins to explore hope, both for the psalmist and for the community of faith, because God is gracious (vv. 5-8).

Significance. Psalm 130, provides liturgical language of hope in situations where human motive is at best mixed and everything appears to go wrong. The opening cry for help in vv. 1-2 underscores how distant God is, while the confession of sin in v. 3 underscores how the consequences of sin go far beyond what any human action could do to improve the situation. These insights bring the psalmist to the ultimate truth that in the end only God can undo our alienation in a broken world—only God can forgive sin. This revelation is the turning point in the psalm, which provides the basis for the soliloquy on hope in vv. 5-8.

New Testament Texts

The lessons continue readings from II Corinthians and Mark. We find ourselves in a new section of the epistle this week, whereas we proceed further through the initial cycle of miracle stories in the Gospel.

The Epistle: *II Corinthians 8:7-15*

A Call to Christian Generosity

Setting. Chapters 8–9 of II Corinthians treat Paul's collection taken among the primarily Gentile-Christian congregations of his missions for the primarily Jewish-Christian congregation of Jerusalem. The Jerusalem church became impoverished because of their boundless generosity in a time of economic hardship and famine, and Paul and his colleagues sought to share the resources of the churches they had founded with those in Jerusalem who had fallen on hard times. In II Corinthians 8 Paul recommends Titus to the Corinthians, discusses the collection, and holds up the Macedonian believers as examples of generosity to the Corinthians (themselves residents of the region Achaia); then, in II Corinthians 9 Paul gives additional information about the collection and tells how he and the Macedonians will come together to the Corinthians to take whatever they have to contribute to the proceeds. The subject is very similar, but the mood of the chapters is distinct: Chapter 8 appeals to the Corinthians, motivating them with information about the generosity of the Macedonians; and chapter 9 makes a further appeal, calling the Corinthians to give as they indicated they would, lest the Macedonians come with Paul and find the Corinthians embarrassingly unprepared.

Structure. The verses of our lesson contain a set of appeals. In vv. 7-12 Paul makes several statements that urge the Corinthians to excel in their generosity. Here, Paul reasons, urges, and explains. His appeal takes a different turn in

vv. 13-15 where he explains that believers are to live in devotion to "equality" with balanced holdings among themselves. He offers a scripture quotation to verify and authenticate his reasoning. The mixture of manners of appeal, the basic principle of "equality," and the use of Scripture indicate how one might form an effective financial appeal today.

Significance. We often find it hard to preach stewardship sermons. In our world there are too many religious hucksters calling for large donations, abusing their contributors' trust, and generally making a mockery of God and Christian faith. No one really wants to be associated with such persons, and so, even when we have legitimate reasons to call on church members for financial support of the life and work of the Church, we find it difficult.

Paul's approach to the Corinthians shows us the lines of a noble, unashamed appeal. Ultimately Paul roots his request in the outlook and will of God. This is clear from his basing the petition on the principle of equality and from his backing the appeal with Scripture. It is in the eyes of God that all believers are equal, certainly not in terms of this world's standards; and Paul and other early believers understood that God's will was discernible from a proper interpretation of the Bible. Thus it does not bother Paul to appeal to the Corinthians (and the other congregations he founded) for monetary contributions, for what they give is according to the will of God, it goes to support the activities that God intends for our lives together in faith.

Paul clearly states the need for which he makes an appeal. Then, he reasons in relation to his request, taking Christ himself as the standard of generosity by which Christians are to measure themselves. Yet Paul issues no commands. He simply states, illustrates, and verifies what God wills for the Corinthians to do. In turn, he trusts that the Corinthians will do what is right because of the reality of their love. Here, Paul's assumptions are powerful. Whatever real love exists in the lives of the

Corinthians is the very love of God, given to the Corinthians by God and sustained among them by the presence and power of God. Thus, when Paul makes an appeal that is in fact God's will, he can count on the Corinthians to comply with the request because God's love present in their lives will respond to God's appeal set before them.

Today, we can take Scripture as our point of departure in making financial appeals. In turn, we can confidently lay out our case, stating why it is according to God's will and calling for a Christ-like response on the part of believers. We may do this work boldly, knowing that a godly appeal made to godly people will be successful because God is at work in the appeal and in the lives of believers to accomplish God's purposes.

The Gospel: *Mark 5:21-43*

Jesus Christ, Lord over Sickness and Death

Setting. The miracle stories of Mark's Gospel offer clear demonstrations of the Lordship of Jesus Christ. Our lesson combines two stories, and together they form the third unit in the cycle of miracles. Readers of the Gospel have seen that Jesus is the Lord of nature (4:35-41) and the Lord over demonic forces (5:1-20), and in our lesson we find that he is Lord over sickness and death.

Structure. Mark employs the literary technique of intercalation again in combining the stories of Jairus' daughter and the hemorrhaging woman. Minor motifs in both stories enhance the "sandwiching" of the accounts: there are two female characters with health problems, Jairus' daughter and the woman Jesus calls "daughter"; the hemorrhage has lasted twelve years and the child is twelve years old; and, above all, though more subtly, the issue of faith is a crucial element of each healing or restoration. Structured in this manner, the stories form commentary on each other: For all practical purposes, the bleeding of this woman rendered her as good as dead in first-century Jewish culture, and the healing she found through her encounter with Jesus was like being brought back from the dead!

Significance. For different reasons the faith of a frightened father and the faith of a despondent woman bring them both to Jesus Christ. Both stories share the generic patterns of Hellenistic miracle stories—problem, action, resolution with confirmation; but they are not accounts about magic or the merely miraculous. In the interactions between Jesus and these characters we learn the true depth and extent of his power. As the faith of the woman leads her to touch Jesus' garment, we find that his power is so great that it brings healing even when Jesus himself is not fully cognizant of its operation. As the faith of the father (and, in turn, mother) leads him to ask Jesus to heal his daughter we find that even when the little girl dies, she is not beyond Jesus' power to restore her.

There are many details in these stories that call for elucidation through careful Bible study. For example, we can learn about Jairus' capacity in the life of the synagogue, the status of the bleeding woman in Jewish life, the practices of ancient medical doctors, the style of garments Jesus would have worn, the role of mourners at Jewish funerals, and so on. All these items will be suggestive for the imaginative employment of this lesson in proclamation, but these are actually peripheral matters rather than the central concerns of the text.

The passage provokes two crucial questions: (1) What is the meaning of *faith,* and (2) who is this Jesus? First, together these stories teach us that genuine faith means recognition, trust, and risk. Both Jairus and the woman with the hemorrhage make their way to Jesus Christ. Having heard of Jesus and finding themselves helplessly in need, they recognize in Jesus the power of God that can and will bring healing and wholeness. Moreover, beyond bare recognition, both Jairus and the woman take action in relation to Jesus, which shows their hopes flower into trust. They turn to Jesus, and in different ways they do what they believe is necessary to bring the power they have perceived to bear on the problems that are marring their lives (and the lives of loved ones). Faith is active, it is not only recognition or intellectual assent, it directs the course of our lives toward the one whom we say we recognize as having the power necessary to restore us to wholeness. Furthermore, faith takes chances. Jairus was a person of stature, and his role as a religious leader could have set him at odds with Jesus—in the same fashion that readers of Mark see other religious leaders relating to Jesus; but, instead Jairus turns to Jesus, risking the health of his daughter and his own relations with other religious leaders who are inclined to say Jesus' power comes from the devil. Similarly, the woman crosses the boundaries of acceptable behavior and makes her way through a pressing crowd secretly to touch Jesus' garment. If she were found out, the reaction of the crowd would be negative; for as she came into contact with them, her condition "defiled" them as it would Jesus whom she intended to touch. Yet, she risked real disapproval, even danger, and made her way to Jesus.

Second, we see Jesus. He clearly has the power to heal and to restore life. His power is astonishing. He knows, even amidst a pressing throng, when he is touched by one calling forth his healing power. His superiority, however, is awesome though not austere; for he summons the woman to commend her, not to reprimand. In turn, in the face of doubts and mocking laughter Jesus raises the little girl; and so, he astonishes her family and his own disciples with a display of his power over death. In Jesus we see the power of God at work in the world for wholeness and life—that is, for salvation which means real peace.

Proper 8: The Celebration

The following is a little known text by William Cowper (famous for the image, "There is a fountain filled with blood") which admirably relates to today's Gospel lesson. Of all the major denominational hymnals, "Heal Us, Emmanuel, Hear Our Prayer" has only appeared in *The United Methodist Hymnal* (no. 266), set to Grafenberg.

Heal us, Emmanuel, hear our prayer;
we wait to feel thy touch;
deep-wounded souls to thee repair,
and Savior, we are such.

Our faith is feeble, we confess
we faintly trust thy word;
but wilt thou pity us the less?
far be that from thee, Lord!

Remember him who once applied
with trembling for relief;
"Lord, I believe," with tears he cried;
"O help my unbelief!"

She, too, who touched thee in the press
and healing virtue stole,
was answered, "Daughter, go in peace:
thy faith hath made thee whole."

Like her, with hopes and fears we come
to touch thee if we may;
O send us not despairing home;
send none unhealed away.

The text is in the public domain and may be reprinted. United Methodist readers may wish to note that the last line of the second stanza above has been altered from the way it appears in their hymnal in order to make the line more singable.

Also related to the Gospel lesson is John Greenleaf Whittier's hymn, "Immortal Love, Forever Full," which appears in some hymnals with the first line "We may not climb the heavenly steeps." It may be found in *The Baptist Hymnal* (SBC, 1991), no. 480; *The Book of Hymns* (United Methodist, 1964), nn. 157-58; *The Hymnal* (Presbyterian, 1933), no. 178; *Hymnal and Liturgies of the Moravian Church,* no. 196; *The Hymnbook* (Presbyterian, 1955), no. 229; *Hymnbook for Christian Worship* (American Baptist and Disciples, 1970), no. 12; *Hymns for the Living Church,* no. 424; and *The Mennonite Hymnal,* no. 150.

Today's epistle lesson, with its emphasis on the collection, may provide a basis for placing the offering after the sermon in order to stress in the liturgy the theological significance of giving in response to the Word. We give because we have become acquainted with God's generous act of sacrifice in Jesus Christ, the living Word. When the offering becomes so unimportant that it is received early in the service purely for the convenience of those who will be counting it, then a congregation's theology of stewardship may need an overhaul because even at the symbolic level, the offering is best presented as an act of sacrifice. Another text of Whittier's may also be employed today at the presentation of the offering:

> All things are thine; no gift have we,
> Lord of all gifts, to offer thee;
> And hence with grateful hearts today,
> Thine own before thy feet we lay.

Old 100th can still be used for this text.

The liturgical placement of the offering also includes the use and place of the Prayer of Dedication. To offer the prayer over empty plates before the offering has been received is to raise a question about what is dedicated. Attentive parishioners might wonder if the tone of such prayers tends to the hortatory, addressed more to the prospective givers than to God. Today's Prayer of Dedication can fittingly reflect the spirit of the epistle, as follows:

> Generous God, you strengthen our love to help us meet the test of others' needs. Receive and use these gifts so that abundance and need may be balanced in the world; through Jesus Christ who became poor for our sake. Amen.

Proper Nine
Sunday Between July 3 and 9 Inclusive

Old Testament Texts

The Old Testament texts present two perspectives on Zion—one historical and one theological. Second Samuel 5 is an account of how David captured Jerusalem, and Psalm 48 provides theological reflection on the meaning of Zion.

The Lesson: *II Samuel 5:1-5, 9-10*

The Capture of Jerusalem

Setting. Second Samuel 5 closes out a cycle of traditions or narratives that began in I Samuel 16 and aimed toward the rise of David. He began as a shepherd boy who tended his father's sheep (I Samuel 16:11) and in II Samuel 5 he is proclaimed the shepherd of all Israel (5:2). The initial cycle of the story of David is enveloped by the image of the shepherd.

Structure. The boundaries of the lectionary text are vv. 1-10. For some reason vv. 6-8 have been eliminated, but these verses should probably be included to make the lesson meaningful and explain David's motives for becoming great. The text separates clearly into two parts: vv. 1-5 describe the choice of David to be king by the northern tribes, and vv. 6-10 describe how David conquered the Jebusite city of Jerusalem, which made him the greatest of Israelite leaders.

Significance. Interpretation will follow the two parts of the text. First, the anointing of David as king over all of Israel in vv. 1-5. David was anointed king over Judah in II Samuel 2:1-7. In II Samuel 2–3 we learn that he ruled the southern kingdom from Hebron, while Saul's son Ishbosheth was made ruler over the northern tribes, and that there was war between the two kingdoms. The final point is significant, for it underscores that the northern and southern tribes are already split by different allegiances prior to the united monarchy. We often think of the split of the kingdoms after David and Solomon as a tragic break up of a people who were previously unified. A closer reading of II Samuel 2–3 suggests a revisionist view of this history, namely that the united monarchy under David and Solomon was not the natural outgrowth of a unified tribal confederacy, but a novel experiment in unity that failed visibly after two kings. Thus the choice of David by the northern leaders in II Samuel 5:1-5 should be interpreted as a radical political move on their part, which is prompted by the assassination of Ishbosheth (II Samuel 4). The language of the tribal leaders in vv. 1-2 has caused some debate by past interpreters. The word *king* (Hebrew, *melek*) is used in the speech of the northern leaders to describe Saul, but David is designated a "chosen leader" (Hebrew, *nagid*—This distinction is nearly lost in the NRSV, which translates *nagid* as "ruler."). Scholars have wondered whether the change of language indicates a tension between northern and southern views with regard to David. In any case David is clearly designated king (Hebrew, *melek*) in v. 3, and the noble experiment in political unity begins.

Second, the conquest of Jerusalem in vv. 6-10. The new kingdom that was formed with the alliance of the northern and southern tribes lacked a capital. Hebron certainly wouldn't do, since it had a tradition of being the capital of the southern kingdom. The transfer of the capital to a northern city like Shechem, Shiloh, or Gilgal also would not work for the same reasons. Verses 6-10 provide a glimpse into the political cunning of David. The Jebusite stronghold of Jerusalem was centrally located in the newly formed kingdom, and it had never been conquered by any Israelite tribe. Thus no Israelite could lay claim to the city, which made it the perfect site for the capital of the united monarchy. The narrative tells us very little, but we learn enough. (1) The city dwellers were overconfident, boasting that the walls were so strong that they could be defended by the blind and lame residents. (2) David and his privately paid soldiers entered the city through the water shaft and conquered it. (3) Jerusalem became identified as the ''city of David,'' making it the symbol of the newly formed kingdom under David. Washington, D.C., provides an analogy for understanding the politics of David's actions. The thirteen colonies had the same problem of competing allegiances, which made Boston, Philadelphia, Richmond, and New York impossible choices for a capital of the newly formed federation. The solution, of course, was to create a city which had no previous tradition in any state, and thus could symbolize the new nation. Jerusalem is much like Washington, D.C., both in the way that it provided a political solution for promoting unity and in the way that it acquired symbolic significance. As a symbol, Jerusalem became known as Zion.

The Response: *Psalm 48*

The Symbol of Zion

Setting. Psalm 48 is a hymn of praise, which is apparently part of a liturgy or festival celebration. Take note of the statement by the worshipers in v. 8: They had heard great things about Zion, but now they actually see it. This statement suggests that those who sing this song are participating in a festival in Jerusalem—perhaps pilgrims coming for a national festival. The imagery of a procession enters again in v. 12 when the worshipers are encouraged to walk about Jerusalem.

Structure. Psalm 48 separates into three parts. Verses 1-3 are a call to praise. The Lord is named in v. 1 before the object of praise shifts to Zion. Thus Psalm 48 praises God indirectly through the symbolism of Jerusalem and its Temple. Verses 4-11 provide the reasons for praise, which are two: Yahweh provides Israel with security by battling the nations (vv. 4-8) and by being present with the people of God in the Temple (vv. 9-11). Verses 12-14 provide a conclusion by calling for a procession around Jerusalem, while proclaiming trust in God's security.

Significance. As the capital of the newly formed united monarchy, Jerusalem and its Temple become a springboard for theological reflection on God's guidance in forming this new state. *Zion* is the word that signifies this shift from politics (David's conquest of a Jebusite city) to theology (God's providence in uniting Israel). Psalm 48 is a key to the theological content that is embedded in the word *Zion*. The imagery of God throughout the psalm is monarchical. God is a king and his kingdom is potentially universal. Verse 2 is especially noteworthy because it describes the rule of God through geographical imagery. God is enthroned in the city of Jerusalem and his kingdom reaches to the ends of the earth. The reference to the far north as the location of God's throne is not a lapse in logic by the writer, but mythological language signifying how God's rule is of a different quality altogether, and thus it is able to be universally present to all people. Such use of geography for the purpose of theology is difficult for modern readers to grasp. Vestiges of this type of language remain in association with Santa Claus. When we tell our children that Santa lives in the far north, we don't mean geography. This becomes painfully clear when children begin to suggest summer trips to meet Santa, and we find ourselves explaining that no matter how far north we travel, he always lives a little farther north. When we use the geographical imagery of the north pole, we are really telling our children that Santa represents a qualitatively different form of life that we all aspire to model: He lives to give things away (he makes presents) and his influence is potentially universal in scope (all children receive them). When the psalmist locates God's throne both in the city and in the far north, the theological claim is that God's rule is potentially universal. Verse 3 turns the focus inward again by stating that such universal power makes Jerusalem secure. The body of the hymn moves between the two poles of God's universal rule over the nations (vv. 4-8) and the security of Zion because of God's presence with the people of God (vv. 9-11), which leads to the statements of trust (vv. 12-14).

Zion is a powerful symbol of salvation in the Old Testament. It embodies claims about divine providence, about God's presence with the people of God, and about the need for the whole world to recognize God's activity. It is also a dangerous symbol because of its concrete claims about God and country. The danger of the symbol is evident in the conclusion to the hymn. If you were a worshiper in ancient Israel and you sang Psalm 48 while you walked around Jerusalem and measured the thickness of its walls and counted its many defensive towers, after a while it would be difficult to separate divine providence from the fortress itself. When this fusion happens, Zion becomes idolatrous and nationalistic, in the attempt to defend holy turf by violent means against any other kind of group. The same danger arises when we construct some of our finest cathedrals in Washington D.C. The reality of Zion must be preached: God rules, God's rule is potentially universal, and God provides absolute security for the people of God by dwelling with them. The reality of Zion, however, must be located in the church and not in the state. Walk around your sanctuary, what do the symbols of its architecture say? Use them in your sermon.

New Testament Texts

Our lessons reflect upon paradoxical contrasts at the core of Christian life. Paul points to the amazing phenomenon of divine power active in the context of human weakness, a reality that reveals the nature of God's gracious power and offers comfort to believers who struggle with less than perfect circumstances in this world. Mark's Gospel shows us Jesus both being rejected by those skeptical of his power and subsequently exercising his authority in clear demonstration of that power.

The Epistle: *II Corinthians 12:2-10*

Divine Strength and Human Weakness

Setting. Many, perhaps the majority of, interpreters regard II Corinthians 10–13 as a fragment of an earlier, longer letter; and even those who regard II Corinthians as a unified document see these chapters as a distinct section of the epistle. From the letter as we have it in the New Testament we learn that Paul paid a painful visit to Corinth (see 12:14 and 13:1) and as a result of that unpleasant experience he wrote a tearful, anguished letter that caused the Corinthians grief (see 2:1-4). Whether chapters 10–13 come from that anguished letter or whether they are part of a later letter may never be settled. But, clearly in this portion of our canonical II Corinthians Paul issues a blistering attack against his opponents in Corinth. He maintains his previous position, namely that his theology and manner of ministry are reflections of the truth of the Christ-event. In general, in II Corinthians 10–13 Paul chews out the Corinthians while defending himself and blasting his opponents.

Structure. In chapter 12 Paul labors to distance himself from the claims and activities of the super-apostles. In the verses of our lesson we find Paul replying to the super-apostles' assertion of their spiritual depth. He tells of his own spiritual experiences, but he does so in a highly ironic fashion indicating that he is not sure about the identity of the spiritual man (himself) whose experiences he reports. First, Paul reports his experience indirectly, saying finally he will only boast of his weakness (vv. 2-5). Then, he writes of his "thorn in the flesh," telling how he prayed for relief, but God gave only sustaining grace. Thus Paul finds his strength in his weakness (vv. 6-10). Finally, in vv. 11-12 (13), Paul bluntly confronts the Corinthians by recalling how he had ministered among them in a striking manner that they should have recognized and remembered.

Significance. There may be no more profound passage in all of Paul's epistles than these verses. They express Paul's theological perspective of "strength in weakness," a theme that permeates the apostle's writings, guiding his thinking in relation to a variety of situations. Previously in II Corinthians 4:1–5:10 the reader of this letter has encountered a lengthy discussion of this perspective, but here the heat of the debate sharpens Paul's manner of expression so that we see the heart of his Christian theology in bold relief.

Through vv. 2-4 the refrain "I do not know; God knows" is sounded. This is Paul's recognition of divine superiority and priority in Christian life. Paul knows of the remarkable spiritual experience of the unnamed man in whose behalf he will boast (himself), but he does not grasp the exact nature of the experience, God does. This thrilling experience is noteworthy, but it is ultimately so nebulous as to serve no concrete purpose. Therefore, Paul does not do theology out of the background of spiritual exaltation.

Indeed, after reporting this enigmatic event, he turns in v. 5 to declare solemnly, "On my own behalf I will not boast, except of my weaknesses." What does he mean? The apostle regards such spiritual experiences as real, but they are essentially private and, therefore, useless for others. Much like the dramatic practice of speaking in tongues, spiritual exaltation may be very edifying for the individual, but these experiences are not the stuff that cultivates the community of faith. The dangerous backside of a preoccupation with dazzling spiritual things is a bent toward personal boasting meant to establish individual spiritual superiority—a problem the Corinthians know all too well.

Thus, Paul continues his argument. In v. 6 he makes it clear that if he wanted to boast, as do others, of high-flown personal spirituality he could; but he boasts of weakness so that others will not be misled into revering him rather than the God and the gospel he preaches. And from vv. 7-10 we learn that to confirm the correctness of Paul's practice of focusing on his own weakness rather than parading his privileged spiritual adventures, he was given a thorn in the flesh. Although Paul regards this difficulty (whatever it was, and no one today knows!) as a satanic entity, he tells the Corinthians that God used it; for when he prayed for relief, God answered, "My grace is sufficient for you, for power is made perfect in weakness." This answer is purely consistent with the reality of Christ who died that God's power could defeat the forces of sin and save humanity. God's grace is sustaining grace. Christian faith is not magic, nor is it a guarantee of glory, especially of personal aggrandizement. In fact, God's true character is seen best in relation to human weakness, for as the power of God sustains us despite our weaknesses, we see plainly that real power is God's, not ours, and that our certitude comes in a sustained relationship to God, not merely from something we get from God.

The Gospel: Mark 6:1-13

From Ridicule and Rejection to Commission and Conquest

Setting. Mark organizes, or inherits stories about Jesus' miraculous mighty works in two cycles of narrative. From 4:35 through 6:6a we find one set of accounts that ends with Jesus' rejection in his hometown despite the mighty works he had done elsewhere. Then, after a two-part interlude in which (1) Jesus sends out the twelve to do ministry and (2) we are informed of

Herod's execution of John the Baptist (6:6b-29), we come to a second series of miracles, which are blended with accounts of Jesus' teachings and debates with religious authorities (6:30–8:21). All these occurrences are located in the Galilean phase of Jesus' ministry prior to his move toward Judea and Jerusalem.

Structure. Our lesson comprises two distinct stories, drawn from two recognizable sections of the Gospel. First, vv. 1-6a recall the situation Jesus faced in his hometown; and, second, vv. 6b-13 recount the mission of the twelve. Clearly either set of verses would make a good text for preaching, and it may prove hard to use the whole lesson in a sermon that would be coherent and of reasonable length.

Significance. Several important lessons are communicated in the verses of the Gospel lesson. First, there is a sharp contrast between the reaction of the hometown crowd to Jesus and the great popularity he had among the throngs in the earlier stories to this point in the Gospel. Like the religious authorities and his family, the hometown people find Jesus less than purely impressive. Indeed, the way Mark tells of their reaction suggests that they found Jesus pretentious, "Who does he think he is anyway?" It is a sad old proverb that familiarity breeds contempt, and while this story tells us that much, it also tells us more. The hometown crowd does not deny that Jesus has done striking mighty works, but since they know exactly who he is, they are incapable of thinking beyond their prejudices to see the gracious power of God present in the familiar.

Second, this initial story brings together the concepts of miracles and faith in a provocative way. One could conclude quite erroneously that miracles depend upon faith, but notice that Jesus did some minor mighty works despite the lack of faith which he found amazing. Rather than the hometown people looking at the person and work of Jesus and being amazed by the goodness of God, we find Jesus looking at the sad incapacity of the crowd and being amazed by their pathetic lack of faith. Faith here is not cast as the medium for miracles but, rather, as the ability to recognize the power of God when it presents itself in our midst. We grasp the real meaning of Jesus' miracles when in faith we perceive, acknowledge, and respond to what God is doing through Jesus Christ.

In the next story Mark follows up on the account of the ridicule and rejection of the hometown people by telling of Jesus' commissioning of the twelve for divinely empowered ministry. Repeatedly in Mark's Gospel we find the pattern of rejection followed by demonstration of authority. In general this pattern, and in particular the two portions of our lesson for this week, come in anticipation of the death and resurrection of Jesus.

Jesus' commissioning of the twelve incorporates them into his own experience, and for disciples of Christ the lesson should be plain: Devotion to God's will and work will lead to confrontation with forces set in opposition to God, and we may experience even brutal rejection; but the final say is God's, so that by God's power even our experience of rejection may eventuate in divine victory according to God's will. Indeed, the victorious power of God, which in Jesus Christ overcame the resistance and hostility of evil, now continues to work through the lives of believers whom Christ commissions to do the work he himself began. And the teaching of Jesus in these verses declares that our faithfulness, especially in the face of resistance, functions as a symbol of God's ultimate judgment of evil.

Proper 9: The Celebration

On this Sunday close to the Fourth of July, the preacher may wish to focus on the Old Testament lesson by asking what is at the heart of a nation. David sought to unite the country around the city that would also be the dwelling place of God. But the lesson gives us an opportunity to make clear how David's success was due to the fact that God was with him and not because of some particular preference that God had for Zion. The subsequent history of Jerusalem and the Temple demonstrates the tragedy of identifying God's presence with some one place and taking that as a guarantee of invincibility and automatic divine favor. Liturgically, this suggests that "Glorious Things of Thee Are Spoken" or "Come, Ye That Love the Lord" ("Marching to Zion") are more appropriate opening hymns than "My Country, 'Tis of Thee" or "America the Beautiful." The function of the opening hymn is to unite the congregation in praise of God, not the nation. Hymns of petition for the nation are fitting later in the service and may be included as part of the prayers.

"Thanks to God Whose Word Was Spoken" may serve either as an opening hymn or between the first two lessons, since the first stanza refers to the calling of Israel and the second stanza (depending upon the hymnal) refers to the grace which is the subject of the epistle lesson. It can be found in *The Book of Hymns* (United Methodist, 1964), no. 18; and *The Hymnal* (Episcopal, 1982), no. 630. In *The Presbyterian Hymnal* (1990) it appears at no. 331 as "Thanks to God Whose Word Was Written," and only the stanza (third) related to grace appears. In this case it would be preferable to use that stanza as a response to the epistle lesson.

The following lines related to the epistle may be sung as a benediction response:

> Be our strength in hours of weakness,
> In our wanderings be our guide;
> Through endeavor, failure, danger,
> Be thou ever at our side. (L. M. Willis, alt.)

The text is in the public domain. Familiar tunes for it include Galilee ("Jesus Calls Us") and Stuttgart.

The following Wesley text, also related to the epistle, may serve as a benediction response (tune: St. Catherine).

> In suff'ring be thy love my peace,
> In weakness be thy love my power;
> And when the storms of life shall cease,
> Jesus, in that important hour,
> In death as life be thou my guide,
> And save me, who for me hast died.

Proper Ten
Sunday Between
July 10 and 16 Inclusive

Old Testament Texts

Second Samuel 6 is the story of how David returned the Ark to Jerusalem. Psalm 24 is a hymn apparently used upon entrance to the Temple.

The Lesson: *II Samuel 6:1-5, 12b-19*

David, the Ark, and Religious Change

Setting. The Ark appears to be an ancient cultic symbol in Israel. Its earliest use is difficult to determine, but it appears to have been firmly established in Israel's worship tradition prior to the Jerusalem Temple. The present narrative, therefore, recounts how these two central aspects of Israel's worship—Ark and Temple—were brought together, and how the combination is not a casual one.

The Ark is described in Exodus 25:10-22; 37:1-9 as being a four-feet-long, two-and-a-half-feet-high, and two-and-a-half-feet-wide box made of acacia wood. The poem in Numbers 10:35-36 provides a glimpse into the earliest function of the Ark as a cult object used in executing a holy war. Writers have placed this old poem in the setting of the wilderness to describe how God led Israel against her enemies:

Arise, O Lord, let your enemies be scattered,
and your foes flee before you.
Return, O Lord of the ten thousand thousands of Israel.

Here the Ark represents God's sole leadership of Israel as well as God's ability to move with Israel and not be located in one place. The Ark also functions in the setting of holy war in I Samuel 4:1*b*–7:1, where it was used unsuccessfully against the Philistines. In fact some scholars suggest that II Samuel 6 is a continuation of the earlier story of the Ark, which has been separated by the present formation of I and II Samuel. The literary connections between II Samuel 6 and I Samuel 4:1*b*–7:1 are not nearly as important to the preacher as the meaning of the Ark for ancient Israel. It represents a confession of God as Israel's sole holy warrior and protector, which are also the roles that David is assuming by becoming king. A story of David bringing the Ark to Jerusalem, therefore, is tension filled, for it is meant to explore the surprising transformations and the accompanying dangers to the community of faith when a tradition moves through time and thus changes.

Structure. Two distinct traditions have been brought together in the present form of II Samuel 6—the bringing of the Ark to Jerusalem and the conflict between David and Michal, Saul's daughter and David's wife. The lectionary text tries to unify these two traditions by skipping vv. 6-11. Therefore, even though v. 16 shifts the focus momentarily to the marital conflict between David and Michal, interpretation will remain with the Ark narrative.

There are good reasons for using the entire narrative of vv. 1-19 for preaching. The unit separates into four parts defined by distinct geographical locations where the Ark travels: vv. 1-5 takes place at the house of Abinadab in Baalejudah; vv. 6-8 at the threshing floor of Nacon, now named Perezuzzah because of David's response to the events that take place there; vv. 9-11 at the house of Obededom the Gittite; and vv. 12-19 in

Jerusalem. The opening (vv. 1-5) and closing (vv. 12-19) sections emphasize the joy of bringing the Ark to Jerusalem by repeating the motifs of dancing and singing (vv. 5, 14), while the middle two sections (vv. 6-8 and 9-11) complicate this story by describing how God killed one of Abinadab's sons, Uzzah, for touching the Ark (vv. 6-8) and David's fearful response to this event (vv. 9-11).

Significance. II Samuel 6:1-19 is a story about change. The writer has been preparing us for drastic social and religious change since I Samuel 8 (Proper 5), when Israel requested a king. The rise and fall of Saul and subsequent rise of David have moved the story along to the point where Israel is no longer the loose tribal confederacy that was soundly defeated twice by the Philistines culminating in the loss of the Ark (I Samuel 4:2–7:1). Instead they are becoming an organized nation with a central leadership, who defeat the Philistines twice (II Samuel 5:17-25), and now find themselves in a position to reclaim the Ark. Thus the story has come full circle. David's decision to retrieve the Ark and to bring it to Jerusalem (his city) sets the stage for a confrontation between the old and the new.

The opening and closing sections (vv. 1-5, 12-19) emphasize the positive characteristics of change, while the middle two sections (vv. 6-8, 9-11) provide a warning. The sequencing of the story is important for interrelating the positive and negative dimensions. Second Samuel 5:17-25 underscore how David has become a successful holy warrior, who "did just as the LORD had commanded him" (II Samuel 5:25). The story of David bringing the Ark from Baalejudah in vv. 1-5 follows immediately from this closing verse. The sequence of events in II Samuel 5 and 6 would suggest that there is no reason to doubt David's motivation in wishing to bring the Ark to Jerusalem. Although two factors in this section raise the question of who is leading whom at this moment of change for Israel.

First, it is worth noting that David is clearly the primary actor here, and that there is no inquiry of whether God actually wants the Ark in Jerusalem. Second, the times have changed from the earlier narratives in which the Ark functions (I Samuel 4:1*b*–7:1). David is not a judge like Samuel, and Israel is no longer simply a tribal confederacy. Consequently, old confessions concerning the character of God's leading that were symbolized in the Ark can never have exactly the same meaning, especially when we remember that the Ark is on its way to "the city of David."

God stops the story in the middle two sections to clear up any ambiguity concerning lingering questions of who is leading whom at the moment of change. The action of Uzzah at the threshing floor of Nacon and David's response of anger suggests that, indeed, there may have been some ambiguity about who was in the driver's seat at this moment. The story is familiar. The cart carrying the Ark is jostled, and Uzzah, one of the sons of Abinadab, appears to offer God a helping hand by holding the Ark. The action is far too casual when dealing with the divine, and he is immediately killed. Note that David's response is not first fear, but anger (vv. 6-8). How could God stop this good thing that he was doing for God? The whole mood of the story changes in vv. 9-11, when David acquires a proper response to divine presence: fear or awe. Fear of God, sometimes renamed as religious awe, prompts David to house the Ark at Obededom where divine blessing begins to emanate for a three-month period. The story starts over in vv. 12-19. Dancing once again becomes a central motif, but the context is far less casual. Sacrifice is first offered after the Ark is moved just six steps, and then again in Jerusalem. The story ends with the old being embodied in something new: The blessing of the ancient Ark is now being mediated through the new king David.

The central focus for preaching II Samuel 6:1-19 is the problem of change. How do we move through time with God? When is change healthy and necessary, and when is it our own manipulation of God? The lectionary text does not provide a complete answer to these questions. Instead it lays out avenues for evaluating change as well as warnings. First, a central component to the narrative is that change is inevitable. The cycle of the larger story in I and II Samuel from Israel's defeat and loss of the Ark to the Philistine's defeat and Israel's reclaiming of the Ark does not bring the reader back to the original starting point. The aim of II Samuel 6 is not to idealize a lost moment in the past, but to push the story ahead into the new setting of Jerusalem. Second, human motivation cannot be the sole criteria for evaluating change in religious tradition. For all we know Uzzah was as highly motivated a Yahwist as is David. But Yahweh kills one and stops the actions of the other when the process of change appears to be too casual—that is, based too much on the self-perceived purity of human motivation. Third, and this would appear to be the central point of the story: Although change in how we worship and what we say about God is inevitable, it must be undertaken with great fear. Paradoxically, such fear only arises from understanding the full power of past tradition. David appears to be highly motivated throughout the story, but he only reaches a point of fear at the end when he sees that the power of God embedded in the Ark is far more than his motivation for doing good. Once this is understood—once David acquires the quality of fear—he embodies change by becoming a new channel for divine blessing.

The Response: *Psalm 24*

An Entrance Liturgy

Setting. Psalm 24 displays strong liturgical characteristics. The language of the psalm suggests a procession that leads into the Temple. This is particularly evident through the questions in vv. 3 and 8. The question in v. 3 concerns who may enter the sanctuary, while v. 8 raises questions concerning the nature of God.

Structure. The psalm clearly separates into three parts. Verses 1-2 are a hymnic section that celebrates the creative power of God and his ownership of all aspects of the world. Verses 3-6 have been characterized as a Torah liturgy, in which the character of worshipers is outlined in a question-and-answer format. Finally, vv. 7-10 are a gate liturgy. Once again the question-and-answer format provides the context for describing the character of the enthroned God.

Significance. Psalm 24 parallels the dramatic development of II Samuel 6:1-19. Both texts are about a procession of God into the sanctuary. Psalm 24 also provides a complement to the lesson, since the austere character of the psalm underscores the majesty of God that was lacking in David's initial attempt to move the Ark, but evident at the close of the narrative.

New Testament Texts

The lessons for this week create a new coupling of texts (Ephesians and Mark), which will be repeated again next week. As is generally the case in ordinary time, the lessons are essentially the result of a sequential scheme of readings, and while there may be thematic parallels between the epistle and the Gospel, these congruencies are not necessarily intentional (though some reflection on the possibility of a relationship between them may inspire the homiletical imagination).

The Epistle: *Ephesians 1:3-14*

Blessing God from Whom All Blessings Flow

Setting. Normally Pauline letters open with a greeting, as Ephesians does in 1:1-2, and then follows a prayerful thanksgiving prior to the beginning of the body of the letter. Ephesians, however, has a blessing of God for the blessings Christians have received (similar to a Jewish *berakah*) in vv. 3-14; and then, vv. 15-23 is the usual thanksgiving prayer report.

Structure. The lectionary reading comprises the verses of the divine blessing. The reading has two large moves with several thoughts or themes in each part:

I. Blessed Be God the Father of Our Lord Jesus Christ—
   A. Who blessed us in Christ
   B. Who chose us in Christ
   C. Who destined us for adoption through Jesus Christ.

And, all of God's activity results in the praise of the glory of God's grace.

II. In Christ Himself Believers Have
   A. Redemption and forgiveness according to grace
   B. Wisdom and insight according to his good pleasure
   C. An inheritance according to God's plan—of which the Holy Spirit is a pledge.

The structure of the thought and the themes registered in the blessing is suggestive for the construction of sermons and portions of worship.

Significance. "Bless God" is a daring doxology in praise of the works of God, which are simply too good to be true. The focus and the context of the "blessing" (read "praise") are set in relation to Jesus Christ. God has worked in and through Jesus Christ who is now Lord of the Christian community in order to "bless" Christian believers. The phrases of Ephesians 1:3-6 form a brief cumulative, explanatory litany of God's blessing: God's blessing is tantamount to God's choosing believers and God's adoption (destining) of believers in Christ.

Before considering the ideas of choosing and destining (Presbyterians should take heart from this passage!), we consider the phrase, "in Christ"; for Ephesians says it is in Christ that believers are "chosen" and "destined for adoption." Small seas of ink have been spent spelling out the significance of "in Christ." Some interpreters take the phrase as a synonym for "in church," while others relate "in Christ" to a form of Christian mysticism. The plain sense of the phrase in Ephesians is spatial. To express this sense of "in Christ" we may paraphrase, "in the context of the new creation established by the powerful grace of God at work in the life, death, and resurrection of Jesus Christ."

The statements that God chose and destined us for adoption "in Christ" make clear that it is by God's work and into God's family that we are brought by God's grace. These lines convey a remarkable message about God, about God's work in Christ; and only secondarily do they provide information about us. The point of this passage is that God works graciously through Christ for our benefit. The author is not interested in defining who is chosen and why, or who is not chosen and why not. The lines are theological, not anthropological, because the good news celebrated here is about God. The gospel has meaning for us, but it is not about us. Therefore, we must be careful with this potent text!

Afterword: The lines from the thanksgiving of the letter, which follow our reading (1:15-18), unpack something of the meaning of God's blessings for us. The prayer asks that God give the believers the gift of intimate comprehension of God. Such understanding is not knowledge that comes through human ingenuity or effort—such as knowledge that comes from studying a math textbook. Rather, Ephesians asks for the gift of God's self-disclosure, which would come as an ever deepening relationship between God and the believers. In relation to God, the life of believers is characterized by the joy of hope and an awareness of the richness of God's grace. Believers have a new attitude, but it is not the result of positive thinking; it comes purely as a gift from God, and it activates a new way of living.

The Gospel: *Mark 6:14-29*

Looking Back in Anticipation of the Future

Setting. Readers are asked to consult the discussion of setting for last week's Gospel text for full consideration of the place of these verses in Mark's narrative. As background to his unit it is helpful to notice that in Mark 3:6 we learned that the Pharisees and the Herodians, the political supporters of Herod Antipas, collaborated to destroy Jesus because of their shared opposition to his ministry and popularity.

Structure. There are two distinct sections to the lesson. First, we learn of the reaction of Herod (Antipas) to hearing about the mighty works Jesus did throughout Galilee. Included along with the report of Herod's awareness and response in relation to Jesus, readers of the Gospel are informed of different popular reactions to Jesus among the people of the region (vv. 14-16). By telling of Herod's suspicion that Jesus was John the Baptist redivivus Mark introduces a flashback in his storytelling to recount how John came to be executed by Herod (vv. 17-29).

Significance. Mark's story of the death of John the Baptist is a fascinating account from a historical perspective, and readers may wish to consult a full-blown scholarly commentary to learn about this story in relation to Greco-Roman history (for example, the well-known Jewish historian Josephus recalls the hostility between the house of Herod, especially Herodias, and John the Baptist). But to limit the viewing of this story to a historical perspective would be to miss many of its riches. For instance, Mark seems to have drawn inspiration for forming his version of the story from I Kings 18–19, where we read of the animosity between Jezebel and Elijah; so that this story shows us the extension, even the fullfillment, of "biblical" history and itself anticipates the description of John the Baptist as Elijah having returned in Mark 9:13!

John the Baptist is a very important figure for Mark, as he apparently was for the thinking of many early Christians. Thus, from the outset of Mark's Gospel we have seen John cast as the divinely appointed forerunner of Jesus. His eschatological perspective, his ministry of preaching, his assembly of disciples, and even his fate are all anticipations of Jesus' own ministry. Now, in the overall scheme of the Gospel, Mark pauses to look back (we read of John's being arrested in chapter 1) to tell a story that, in fact, points ahead to the fate Jesus will suffer in the hands of political authorities. In a sense, then, this story is a forceful reminder of the manner in which humans choose to deal with God's appointed representatives. Thus, Jesus himself tells the bitter parable of the vineyard and the tenants (Mark 12:1-11) on the heals of a debate with the authorities about the source of his and John's authority (Mark 11:27-33).

Mark clearly has a high regard for John the Bapist, but still in relation to the other Gospel writers he devotes a disproportionate amount of attention to telling of the Baptist's death. Yet, when we evaluate the significance of this narrative in relation to the gospel story of Jesus, we begin to grasp why Mark gave this volume of space to recalling John's fate. The two parts of our lesson offer a crucial lesson. Mark reports the perceptions and suspicions of both Herod and the people regarding Jesus' mighty works, and in their speculations that he is "John the Baptist," or "Elijah," or "a prophet as of old" we see that they are merely reacting to his ability to do miracles. Yet in John's execution we see the foreshadowing of Jesus' own death, and thus, Mark reminds us that the power to do miracles is not the true significance of Jesus; rather, we truly grasp the meaning of the person and work of Jesus when we focus on his death on the cross. For Mark, the cross is the key to comprehending Jesus Christ. Only when we know him crucified, giving his life as a ransom for many, do we understand who he is. The Son of God who gives his life for others, for us, is the one to whom Mark directs our attention. We may be duly impressed with his power, but we fail to comprehend him unless we think of him, above all, as the one who suffered in order to serve and save others.

Preaching this passage may be tricky. Reflection on John the Baptist should initiate but not dominate the proclamation. The real issue is, "How do you evaluate Jesus?" Do you focus on his power and his miracles—thinking of him as simply divine? Or, do you see him as he lived and died—in saving service to humanity—thereby showing us the real meaning of godliness and the real character of God?

Proper 10: The Celebration

For those churches that prefer to space baptisms more evenly throughout the year in order to provide time for catechetical instruction of baptizands and/or sponsors, the Ephesians lesson today provides a warrant for a mid-summer observance. The references to being in Christ and marked with the seal of the Holy Spirit as well as being adopted as God's children suggest the practice of baptism and baptismal anointing.

If the beheading of John the Baptist is taken as the day's primary text, the opening prayer or collect of the day might be adapted from one by Thomas Cranmer, as follows:

> Almighty God,
> your servant John the Baptist
> prepared the way for the advent of your Son:
> Help us to follow his example
> by constantly speaking the truth,
> boldly rebuking vice,
> and patiently suffering for the truth's sake;
> through Jesus Christ our Lord.

The following form of Psalm 119:46, 48 will serve as a responsive call to worship:

> I will speak of your decrees before kings:
>   and shall not be put to shame.
> I revere your commandments, which I love,
>   and I will meditate on your statutes.

The sermon hymn may be "Am I a Soldier of the Cross" or any other hymn that relates to the cost of Christian witness.

The commentary on the Old Testament lesson makes clear once again the problems that arise when we attempt to condense a longer biblical narrative into shorter portions. The dynamic relationship between the parts is lost, in part, one suspects, because of a late twentieth-century reluctance to deal with those sections of Scripture that portray God in a posture embarrassing to our sensibilities. So last week the omission of the references to the blind and lame causes the reading to place David in charge of Jerusalem with no indication as to how he got there. And this week, to avoid the unpleasantness that happened to Uzzah, the lesson is so divided as to make it impossible to understand how we get from David dancing before the Ark (v. 5) to David fetching the Ark from the house of Obededom (v. 12*b*). As the commentary implies, it may well be that the most important part of the narrative has been omitted! If a lay study group is working with the lectionary texts, there is little doubt that they will read the connecting verses and that it will be to those that their interest is drawn. Reason enough for the preacher to take time with it.

As Psalm 24 is an entrance hymn, so the metrical version based upon it, "Lift Up Your Heads, Ye Mighty Gates," may be used as today's opening hymn or for the psalm itself.

Proper Eleven
Sunday Between
July 17 and 23 Inclusive

Old Testament Texts

Second Samuel 7 is the story of David's desire to build God a Temple, which develops into a promise of election from God that he would build David a house. Psalm 89:20-37 reviews the divine promises to David.

The Lesson: *II Samuel 7:1-14a*

A Promise with a Twist

Setting. Second Samuel 7 is a well-known text. It is the narrative that establishes God's unconditional promise to David that a member of his house would rule Israel forever. This promise is the starting point of messianic theology in ancient Israel. It is central to Christianity because Jesus is confessed to be the fulfillment of the messianic promise to David. With the central role that this text has assumed in Christian tradition, we often neglect to read it very closely once we have made the connection between the messianic promise to David and Jesus. The text certainly presents the messianic ideal, but it does it with a twist.

Structure. Second Samuel 7:1-14a separates into two parts.

I. David's Plan to Build God a House (vv. 1-3)
II. God's Response (vv. 4-14a)
   A. The first speech (vv. 4-7)
   B. The second speech (vv. 8-14a)

Significance. Second Samuel 7 appears on the surface to be a simple narrative. Yet when we look at the motifs and characters that enter these few verses, the complexity is rich and overwhelming. Most of the major symbols and problems of ancient Israelite faith are included: king, prophet, Ark, Temple, blindness (pious motivation to do something for God and prophetic approval which in fact does not represent God's wishes), revelation, power, and election. How do all of these motifs interrelate?

The beginning of the story is important. It opens with David, who is not named, but, instead, is described only with the title, "the king." The use of this title twice in vv. 1-3 is a red flag. The larger story of the rise of the monarchy (Joshua, Judges, Samuel, Kings) makes it clear that the installation of a king in Israel presents a variety of religious problems. The central problem is stated in I Samuel 8:6-9, when Israel requests a king for protection against the Philistines, and God informs Samuel that such a request is not a rejection of Samuel, but of God as king (see the commentary for Proper 5). We learn three things about the king in vv. 1-3: he is dwelling in a house, God has given him peace, he desires the Ark of God also to be in a house, and his piety is sincere (the prophet tells us as much with the closing remark, "The LORD is with you"). The last point is very important. Piety permeates the opening verses. The king's intentions appear to be pure, which prompts (the somewhat unusual) immediate prophetic agreement that the king should build God a temple. Yet this is the dangerous aspect of the story, because housing the Ark (the central symbol of the God of the

Exodus) in a permanent temple has implications that go beyond the pious intentions of the king. Kings and temples frequently go together in the ancient Near East to create a civil religion in which the king is viewed as nearly divine, or at the very least as God's primary representative on earth. In such situations God and state become so intermingled precisely because of the religious and civil role of the king, which creates all kinds of problems concerning whose power is really being worshiped.

Although the topic of conversation between king and prophet has been religious, it is important to note that God has actually been absent from the opening scene. When God does enter at v. 4, however, he virtually takes over the story with two revelatory speeches that provide a response to the pious intentions of king and prophet. The introduction of formal categories of revelation to the prophet Nathan ("Thus says the LORD . . .") underscores the absence of divine inquiry in the opening section. The first speech calls into question the prophet's too easy support of the king by reviewing God's past activity with Israel. The God of the Exodus is not tied to a temple and has never asked for one (vv. 6-7). The second speech focuses more explicitly on the king. Here, God reviews David's rise to power as a divine gift (vv. 8-11a) and concludes this summary by reversing David's wish. Instead of David building God a house, God declares that he would build David a house.

The two parts of the story—David's wish to build God a temple and God's reversal of this wish—must not be interpreted as being directly in conflict, but they are in tension. It is the tension between the two parts of the story that provides an avenue for preaching this text. Our confessions of election frequently arise out of contexts that resemble the opening scene of the story. We are secure in our power and life-style, we are feeling thankful and pious about the good things that we presently experience, and in light of this we wish to do something for God. This is what David is doing at the outset of II Samuel 7, and the prophet Nathan even agrees. God's response to David and Nathan is that they really cannot do anything for God no matter how pious their motives. In this context, the promise of election to David states just the opposite, that God has done and will continue to do tremendous things for David. The promise of election in II Samuel 7 is certainly worthy of celebration, but we must also see that in its larger context it also implies a criticism of our own sense of power of well-being, which we too frequently mistake as the content of God's election. The story achieves this second point by contrasting revelation (the second part of the story) with well-intended piety (the first part of the story).

The Response: *Psalm 89:20-37*

An Oracle of Election

Setting. Psalm 89 is an extended reflection on the Davidic monarchy. The psalm separates into three parts. Verses 1-18 are a hymn celebrating the steadfast love of God. The images for celebrating this divine quality include the election of the Davidic monarchy (vv. 3-4) and creation (vv. 5-18). Verses 19-37 are a divine oracle to the Davidic king, which reviews the divine election of David. Finally, vv. 38-51 are a lament over the decline of the Davidic monarchy. This over emphasizes how Psalm 89 takes up a variety of genres including hymn, oracle, and lament. Commentators suspect a history of tradition to the present formation of the psalm. Verses 1, 2, 5-18 appear to be a hymn celebrating the power of God in creation. Verses 3, 4, 19-37 are a royal poem. And vv. 38-51 might very well be a separate lament.

Structure. The lectionary text is made up primarily of the royal poem, although vv. 20-37 lack the introduction to this section in v. 19, where it is stated that what follows is a vision. There is no clearly discernible structure within the section.

Significance. Psalm 89:20-37 reviews the essential components to the theology of divine election of the Davidic monarchy. The king is the anointed of God (v. 20), which implies protection (vv. 21-23), adoption (vv. 26-27), and covenant—both as the promise of continuous rule (vv. 34-37) and as the responsibility to follow divine statutes (vv. 28-33).

New Testament Texts

Both lessons present a challenge for preaching and worship, for it is impossible to grasp and to articulate the full sense of either passage. While the texts are different in focus and in style, both have an elegant but enigmatic quality that points beyond the mere words on a page to a profound divine reality that embraces us and calls us to celebrate the transforming grace of God that enriches our lives through our encounter with God's work in Jesus Christ.

The Epistle: *Ephesians 2:11-22*

What Is the Church?

Setting. We return to Ephesians 2 in Year B after treating it last during Lent. The epistle seems unrelated to any specific situation, but it is clearly concerned with every divine and human moment. The epistle falls into two broad parts: chapters 1–3 are an elaborate, profoundly theological statement, almost esoteric in nature they are so lofty, complex, and elegant; chapters 4–6 are also evaluated in style, expression, and outlook, but in this portion of the letter we find statements about the ordering of the everyday life of believers. The theme of this epistle, in both its theological and practical parts, however, is cosmic reconciliation.

Structure. Our text is a complex series of statements concerned with juxtaposing two thoughts: Those whom the letter addresses were (a) once far from God, but they are (b) now near in the unity of Christ. The point of view is clearly cosmic, declaring the nature of the Church universal. The passage falls into three parts: First, vv. 11-13 establish the "once/now" scheme, which contrasts the past with the present in terms of being "without Christ" and "in Christ." Second, vv. 14-18 practically give hymnic expression to the idea of "Christ our peace" through whom once estranged but now united portions of humanity (Jews and Gentiles here) have access through "one Spirit to the Father." And third, vv. 19-22 make a summary statement about the meaning of sainthood using the metaphor of the "household of God" to declare that the spiritually unified Church is indeed "a dwelling place for God." While the reflection is highly ecclesiological, we should not allow our thinking about the Church to supersede the profound and crucial Christology, pneumatology, and theology inherent in this text.

Significance. If we put the question, What is the Church? to most people today we will most likely get answers framed in architectural or sociological terms. *Church* typically suggests buildings and social clubs, even if the buildings are regarded as sanctuaries and the social clubs are thought to deal with piety and religious tradition. Read our epistle lesson and try to imagine what the author of Ephesians would think of such assessments of the Church.

Ephesians states its understanding of the Church in many ways, several of which are found in this lesson; but, in a nutshell, Ephesians regards the Church as the result of God's reconciling work in Jesus Christ. Specifically in our lesson Ephesians thinks of the Church as formerly fractured humankind brought together by being brought to God through the atoning death of Christ. Humanity's condition is now different from its state prior to God's work through Jesus Christ. Ephesians here declares a miracle, a mystery, a momentous event of immense magnitude that has real meaning in the real world; yet, because this marvelous accomplishment is the very work of God, it is more celebrated than explained. Thus the author employs multiple metaphors to speak of reconciliation. While the reader encounters no mechanical explanation of the operation of reconciliation, God's meaning in bringing about this wonderful new condition is clear: God worked through the death of Jesus Christ. The mention of Christ's blood points to the power of Christ's life poured out as an act of grace to establish God's covenant with humanity. Though we were ostracized from one another and from God, now God in Jesus Christ has done for us what we could not do for ourselves, God has reconciled us to one another and to God.

The outcome of God's work is that our lives have a new quality and a new purpose. Because of Jesus Christ we have peace. Peace is a biblical notion of utmost importance. We typically reduce our definitions of *peace* to "the absence of strife," but the biblical notion of peace is far more. The peace of God is wholeness of person and relations. It is God's intended mode of human existence, and it means that we are healthy and whole in ourselves, in our friendships and associations with all other human beings, and in our relationship with God. In turn, the purpose of our lives is established through God's reconciling work. Ephesians says we are God's household, a holy temple, a dwelling place for God. This means that the presence and power of God, God's Holy Spirit, infuse us so that we become God's own family, God's abode. God reconciles our flesh and blood and claims it as his own, so that we are those among whom and through whom God moves and works in the world. We must not confuse ourselves with God, but we should see that through Jesus Christ and by the Holy Spirit, God gives us access to God's own self and that, in so doing, God takes access through us to the world.

The Gospel: Mark 6:30-34, 53-56

God's Sufficient Grace in Jesus

Setting. Readers may refer to the discussion of setting for the Gospel lesson for Proper 9 to see the general narrative location of this Sunday's text. We should notice immediately that by leaping over vv. 35-52 the lectionary suggests the omission of both the account of the feeding of the five thousand and the story of Jesus' walking on the water. Instead of these two vivid, memorable events the suggested lesson leaves us to deal with Mark's narration (which is almost abstract) of Jesus' encounter with the throngs. Instead of specific stories we deal with the statement of Jesus' compassion on the crowd, which led to his teaching and healing.

Structure. Even in its abstractness, Mark's narration has the major elements of a stock ancient miracle story. Thus, Mark's readers would understand that they were encountering a remarkable account, and one they were prepared to read. A "standard" ancient miracle story comprised three elements. First, the problem was recognized; second, some action produced extraordinary results; and third, recognition or confirmation of the results was offered.

Our lesson modifies and elaborates the stock miracle form. In the lines leading to the account of the feeding of the five thousand we learn of the return of the disciples from their successful mission, and we find Jesus inviting them to come away alone from the active and demanding crowd. Then, we hear about the frustration of their plans because of the crowd. The context of demand and frustration is set, and yet, in the face of such difficulties we learn of Jesus' compassion. The compassion takes the concrete forms of teaching (vv. 30-34) and healing (vv. 53-56).

Significance. Mark recalls the motive and the means of the ministry of Jesus. Examination of the details of the narrative find repeated christological pointers. Initially we learn of the disciples' return to Jesus. Moved by the news of their success in teaching and healing—that is, in combating the forces of evil, Jesus seeks to withdraw alone to a deserted place. This is the same kind of place where he was tempted at the outset of his ministry. Moreover, this was the kind of place where Israel wandered for forty years, sustained by manna from heaven. In spite of Jesus' desires and efforts to get away, however, the crowd follows and seemingly prevents him from finding the desired solitude. Yet, when Jesus views the crowd, he has compassion; and his concern was more than passive. Jesus taught the multitude. If Jesus is supposed to look a lot like God in this story—as God's Son—then we learn that we cannot wear God down with our problems, and we cannot exhaust God's gracious power.

Notice that the two segments of the lesson frame powerful and important specific stories, the feeding and the walking on the water. In this desert context we should see that in the person and work of Jesus we are seeing the will and the action of God. As God in compassion led the children of Israel out of Egypt, so Jesus teaches the throngs; as God fed Israel in the wilderness, so Jesus feeds the crowd, and as the Israelites in worship celebrated the saving power of God over the sea (see Psalm 107:23-30), so Mark recalls Jesus' comforting the struggling disciples on the sea. We learn from Mark that the power for the work Jesus did is the very power of God. Jesus' work is ultimately God's work. And, through these bits of story and the other accounts between, we are assured that God's provisions are more than enough for our needs.

Proper 11: The Celebration

Today's preacher should note how the image of the Temple appears in both the Old Testament and epistle lessons. In each case the Temple is the work of God. In the first instance the temple built by Solomon does not endure, being the work of human hands. In the second God's people become the temple, and the son of David, Jesus Christ, is the cornerstone. This should remind us that the Greek word for church, *ekklesia*, means "assembly," not "building." Christians, at least in the United States, are inclined to what might be called "templing," or to what some have called an "edifice complex." Most pastors can testify to the comparatively greater ease with which money can be raised for brick and mortar items as opposed to

119

the alleviation of human suffering. A ride through the center of many cities provides a vivid illustration of what becomes of those ecclesiastical monuments when their curators flee to the suburbs and ignore the spiritual building blocks lying derelict against the locked iron gates. Percy Bysshe Shelley's nineteenth-century poem "Ozymandias" takes on a trenchant contemporaneity.

> I met a traveler from an antique land,
> Who said: Two vast and trunkless legs of stone
> Stand in the desert . . . Near them, on the sand,
> Half sunk, a shattered visage lies, whose frown,
> And wrinkled lip, and sneer of cold command,
> Tell that its sculptor well those passions read
> Which yet survive, stamped on these lifeless things,
> The hand that mocked them, and the heart that fed:
> And on the pedestal these words appear:
> "My name is Ozymandias, king of kings:
> Look on my works, ye Mighty, and despair!"
> Nothing beside remains. Round the decay
> Of that colossal wreck, boundless and bare
> The lone and level sands stretch far away.

The Ephesians text, with its emphasis on the apostles and prophets, can serve to call us back to first principles, to the understanding that the Church is a historically conditioned institution that emerged from objective, articulated historical events involving real people. Because most Protestants have rejected a particular theory of apostolic succession (namely, through a line of bishops), they have concluded that apostolic succession is not important, and so have little sense of how they are connected to the original revelatory event. One answer at least has to do with the reading of Scripture and preaching. Faithful reading of Scripture accompanied by preaching that has been undergirded by rigorous exegesis of the texts and of the homiletical context is for Protestants how we stay in dialogue with the church of the apostles, how we stay in apostolic succession.

The following collect, based upon the epistle lesson, is suggested for today's opening prayer.

Almighty God, you have built your Church upon the foundation of the apostles and prophets, Jesus Christ himself being the chief cornerstone: Grant us so to be joined together in unity of spirit by their teaching, that we may be made a holy temple acceptable to you; through Jesus Christ our Lord. (*The Book of Common Prayer*, p. 230)

Hymns for today may include
"Built on the Rock the Church Doth Stand"
"Christ Is Made the Sure Foundation"
"I Sing a Song of the Saints of God"
"Rejoice in God's Saints"
"The Church's One Foundation"
"We Are the Church"

Proper Twelve
Sunday Between
July 24 and 30 Inclusive

Old Testament Texts

Second Samuel 11 is the story of David and Bathsheba. Psalm 14 is a lament over the foolishness of evil.

The Lesson: *II Samuel 11:1-15*

David's "Watergate"

Setting. In the opening chapters of I Samuel, Hannah sang about the power of God to initiate salvation as radical reversals in life. God can bring the arrogant low and break the bows of the mighty (I Samuel 2:2-4*a*), and he can strengthen the weak and feed the hungry (I Samuel 2:4*b*-5*a*). The message of this song has been illustrated by the way in which characters have been paired in contrasting situations (Peninnah-Hannah, Eli-Samuel, Saul-David). David has been on the rise since I Samuel 16, but his fortunes reverse in II Samuel 11, when he becomes too secure in his own power.

Structure. The narrative separates clearly into four sections: an introduction (v. 1), David and Bathsheba (vv. 2-5), David and Uriah (vv. 6-13), the disposal of Uriah (vv. 14-15).

Significance. David's illicit sex with Bathsheba in II Samuel 11 is a well-known story. The familiarity of this story, however, becomes an obstacle for interpreting it, because sexual desire is not the central motif of the narrative. The central theme when preaching this text is the danger of power, and the author alerts us to this central theme in the opening verse. One of the primary reasons for David's stellar rise in power has been his uncompromising commitment to risk all in order to be God's holy warrior. This quality was characterized starkly when David killed Goliath, because the giant dared to offend God. Thus the David and Goliath story follows the overarching pattern of reversal in which God brings the arrogant giant low and raises up the humble David. Many other stories could also illustrate this point about David, and, in view of this, v. 1 jumps off the page. "It is the spring of the year," the author tells us, "the time of the year when kings go out to battle." Holy war is not over for Israel, since the Ammonites still remain in the land. But as we learn at the close of the verse, holy war is over for David. He has become secure in his political power as king, so secure that he sends his general Joab to wage holy war, while he lounges in Jerusalem. After v. 1 it is clear to the reader that what ever follows next will be negative.

Verses 2-5 show the results of David's arrogance in quick fashion. This section moves rapidly from late afternoon voyeurism (David watching Bathsheba bathe) to sexual curiosity (David sends someone to inquire about the beautiful woman) to lovemaking, and finally to pregnancy. The illicit sexual tryst provides the backdrop for vv. 6-13, which is meant to address the central issue of the chapter. The pregnancy must be covered up, which initially strikes the king as only a minor problem. He gives the husband an unexpected furlough and encourages the man to have sex with his wife: "Go to your house and wash your feet" (v. 8, with *feet* being a euphemism for *genitals*). The only problem is that Uriah, the Hittite, understands holy war and refuses to have sex with his wife while Israel is still at risk. His speech in v. 11 is an indictment against the description of David from v. 1. With God (the Ark) and Israel in the pitch of battle, Uriah ironically swears by

David, that he would not enter his house and sleep with his wife. The remainder of the story is denouement. David tries one more time to get Uriah to sleep with Bathsheba by getting him drunk, but it doesn't work (vv. 12-13). So he sends the unsuspecting holy warrior back to the battle front carrying his own death orders (vv. 14-15). End of story.

Second Samuel 11:1-15 is a story about the abuse of power. The most flagrant abuse of power occurs in v. 1, where David shifts from leading Israel, no matter what the risk, to governing the empire. Once he violates this fundamental trust, nearly everything he does accentuates his evil. He violates the laws of holy war by not going. He abuses power by summoning Bathsheba and then again by having sex with her (Deuteronomy 22:22). He may also have violated sexual purity laws (see v. 4 and Leviticus 15:24). Finally he is reduced to a murderer.

The Response: *Psalm 14*

Meditation on the Fool

Setting. The language of Psalm 14 is striking. It begins with a quotation from the fool (Hebrew, *nabal*) that "There is no God." The psalm then proceeds to describe the character of such a person and his or her eventual outcome. The psalm is difficult to categorize. The reflection on the nature of the fool suggests insight from the wisdom tradition. The overall mood of the psalm is one of lament, yet the way in which the lament is voiced has prompted scholars to emphasize a prophetic background for the psalm. Another puzzling characteristic of Psalm 14 is that it reappears in the psalter as Psalm 53 with slight variations (most notable the use of "the Lord" in Psalm 14 as compared to "God" in Psalm 53). See other commentaries for more detailed comparison between these two psalms.

Structure. The psalm can be structured in two different ways. One way is to divide vv. 1-6 and 7, with the former being a wisdom lament and the latter verse expressing hope for an anticipated deliverance. Another way is to separate vv. 1-4, 5-6, and 7. This three-part structure takes into account a shift in mood in vv. 5-6 where the psalmist predicts the outcome of the foolish person.

Significance. Verse 1. Foolishness is a moral category in this psalm rather than an intellectual one. The fool doesn't lack intelligence. The fool lacks moral vision. Such blindness prompts a practical atheism. Practical atheism is not about theoretical doubts concerning the meaning of the cosmos and God's place in it (if any). Rather it signifies a pragmatic attitude about the active presence of God in relationship to everyday activities. The fool does not believe that God is an active force in concrete events. Such a conclusion makes the fool a distortion of humanity. The description of the fool as "corrupt" (Hebrew, *šaḥat*) is the same word used to describe humanity just prior to the flood. Because the fool is in essence distorted, all the fool's actions are also perverted. Nothing good can come from a fool. Verse 1 leaves us with the obvious question: Who are these fools in our midst?

Verses 2-4 provide the answer. Note that it is not the psalmist who provides the answer but God. Foolishness is defined from a divine perspective. (This shift to the divine voice is what has prompted scholars to place the psalm in the prophetic literature.) The divine answer to the question is that all humanity is potentially foolish. The fool is not the exception, but the rule. Foolishness is a universal state of affairs, which prompts the divine speech in v. 4, framed as a question: Have they no knowledge?

Verses 5-6. The voice of the psalmist returns in these verses to affirm the activity of God among the people of God, and to predict the outcome of the foolish, before the psalm ends in v. 7 with an anticipation of divine deliverance.

Clearly the psalm provides commentary on the story about David and Bathsheba. The actions of David provide a poignant example of practical atheism. But the psalm goes beyond the

Old Testament lesson to underscore how the activity of David is all too often characteristic of humanity in general. Foolishness is a universal commodity and a bad investment.

New Testament Texts

We continue the series of readings from Ephesians and turn to the first of five sequential Gospel lessons drawn from John 6. The texts have little in common. The verses from Ephesians are a set of formal expressions of Christian devotion and the text from John is a pair of stories about Jesus' miraculous activity.

The Epistle: *Ephesians 3:14-21*

How Then Shall We Pray?

Setting. Readers may refer to the discussion of setting for Proper 11 to see the general literary location of this lesson. The verses come at the end of the first major section which offers theological perspectives on reconciliation. Chapters 2–3 treat the theme of the meaning of salvation for the present life of the one, unified Church. The verses of our lesson are prayerful in tone, although they have clear didactic value for the readers.

Structure. There are two distinct parts to our lesson: Verses 14-19 report the author's reverent prayer that the recipients of the epistle may know and experience fully the all-surpassing love of Christ; verses 20-21 are a doxology to the all-powerful and gracious God who works through Christ Jesus to form and shape the Church. While the moves and moods of the passage are prayer and praise, the lines of the verses offer many pointers about the content and manner of Christian prayer. Attention to the pattern and property of thought in this lesson may give pointers for the structure and substance of sermons.

Verses 14-19 are one long sentence in Greek, highly polished in vocabulary and cast in carefully constructed rhetoric.

Verses 14-15 report the fact of prayer and name the God to whom the prayer is directed. Then, in verses 16, 18, and 19 we find three clauses of differing lengths which report the purposes of the prayer in three "in order that" statements (Greek: *hina*; translated "in order that," "that," and "so that" in NRSV). The thought of verses 20-21 is not so carefully delineated, though the praise is pointedly directed to the one who "is able to accomplish abundantly far more than all we can ask or imagine," a description which specifically looks back to the three "in order that" clauses.

Significance. Before concluding the first major portion of Ephesians with a doxology to God, the author formulates a complex petition to God which reveals that God desires to enable the readers to experience the fullest form of a truly Christian life. The prayer report begins with a reference to the author's bent knees. It is instructive to recall that the normal posture for prayer in antiquity was standing. Bowing to one's knees was to take the posture of humble, reverential submission assumed before a conqueror; it was to acknowledge another's superiority and to declare one's own loyalty. Bowing before God for prayer is itself a declaration of one's recognition and submission to God's Lordship, largely thought of in terms of power and capacity to rule (thus, the manner of naming God in verse 20!). Assuming this worshipful posture, the author prays.

The first petition is that God will work through the Holy Spirit to strengthen the dimensions of the believers' lives ("you" throughout this passage is plural) which have been redeemed through God's work of reconciliation. In reconciliation God carved out and claimed a new humanity by overcoming the factious forces of sin that fracture our lives into less than God intends for them to be. The author adds a crucial qualifier to the request—that is, that God's work of strengthening the believers be done "according to the riches of his glory." In other words, the strengthening is a benefit to the believers, but it is not a new power that sets us up so much as it

127

sets us in line with God's will. Reconciliation means harmony, unity and peace—for us and with God.

The second petition relates to the indwelling of the believers by Christ. As Christ lives in the members of the community of faith, they find their sustenance, security, and strength in the power of Christ's own selfless love. When Christ is alive in the lives of the believers, they are themselves ("all the saints") brought to a new awareness of the magnitude of God's purposes for life. This transformation has about it a mystical (not magical) quality, so that the author moves to the metaphor of space to describe the vastness of the quality of life in the community of God's reconciliation.

Third, the author concludes the petitions on an enigmatic note, asking that the believers "may be filled with all the fullness of God." Commentators debate the sense of this phrase. Some argue that "all the fullness of God" means "all the gifts that God desires to give you"; but others see a less exact but more profound idea—namely, "with God himself." Since the prayer seems to be mounting to a peak—from strengthening to indwelling to all fullness, and from the Spirit to Christ to God—there is much to be said for the latter interpretation. Thus, the author may pray ultimately for the real unity of the believers with God himself, so that God lives out his will and life through their life as a reconciled community of faith. In any case, inherent in this prayer is an impressive expression of the author's conviction that God's will for believers is an ever-increasing life of godliness brought into existence by God's work in the life of the community of faith. For this, to God be the glory!

The Gospel: *John 6:1-21*

Encounter the Awesome Power of God in Jesus Christ

Setting. The stories in our lesson come from the first two of several loosely related sections in John 6. Although the text is clearly colored with John's language, concerns, and themes, the materials in this chapter of John are remarkably similar in subject and sequence to portions of Mark 6 and 8; so that many interpreters suggest a very primitive early Christian story-cycle lies behind the Gospels' versions of these events.

Structure. Our lesson has two main parts. Verses 1-15 recount the feeding of the five thousand, a story found in the other Gospels, and there are Johannine touches throughout the telling. For example, in verses 14-15, John explains why Jesus left his disciples and went away alone. Then, in verses 16-21 we find the first of two related units concerning the boat trip across the Sea of Galilee to Capernaum. (Verses 22-24 build on the trip per se by telling of the curiosity of the crowd upon finding Jesus on the other side of the sea when he had gone off alone with no boat to bring him over.)

Significance. The story of the feeding of the five thousand is simply too good to be true, or, better, too good not to be true! Explanations that approach this text on the level of sheer history can never grasp its meaning. Certainly some moment in the ministry of Jesus lies behind this text, but in preserving the moment and retelling the story, John and other early Christians (compare the parallel versions in the other Gospels) told the story so that it became a vehicle for the good news of God's work in Jesus Christ. Nineteenth-century interpretations regularly rationalized the miracle by suggesting that the people in the crowd had food up their sleeves or in their pockets (as first-century Jews traveling away from home often did) which they were unwilling to share with others until they witnessed and were moved by Jesus' own generosity. Thus, the story was thought to be a lesson in generosity. But, such interpretations are sheer speculation and simply fall short of the sense of the account. Indeed, this story is more concerned with Jesus and his work than with issuing moral lessons.

Examination of the details of the narrative finds the repeated christological pointers. Jesus himself recognizes the problem, the lack of food. He turns the problem of the crowd into a problem for the disciples who are not able to resolve the matter; and so, Jesus takes charge, knowing all along what he would do. Now, he gives the disciples an order—they are to cause the crowd to be seated. Then, with the little bit of food in hand, Jesus is clearly in control. The action advances as Jesus turns to God in thanksgiving. The power for the work Jesus did is clearly God's. And, as we see, God's provisions in Jesus Christ are more than enough for our needs.

In turn, we have the story of Jesus' walking on the water. There are a variety of ways to approach this passage for proclamation. Whichever path one takes, there are two basic strategies to make the sermon "work." First, avoid getting into the "science" of this story. Past generations of interpreters often gave rationalizing explanations of the account—Jesus was only up to his ankles in shallow water, or Jesus knew where the reef was that ran off the shore just beneath the water and he was walking on top of it, or this is a post-Easter story that was mistakenly placed in the context of Jesus' ministry prior to his death and resurrection, and so on. Such interpretations explain away the power of this narrative and refuse to admit that this story goes beyond what most people are prepared to believe or are able to understand. In the same way, sermons that say, "I don't know whether he walked on the water, but I do know that he came to me in the struggles of my life," sell short the profundity of this passage. Second, notice how John crafted this story and try to capture some of the brilliance of the text in your own sermon. Do not hesitate to preach a powerful and dramatic sermon on this lesson, and since the story is laden with images and details, turn to art for images and illustrations.

Above all, this story is about the authority of Jesus. In verses 14-15 Jesus recognizes the intentions of the crowd and left them (out of disapproval of their plan); Jesus exercises authority over the elements of nature, both in walking on the water and in miraculously moving the boat to its destination; and Jesus speaks with confidence and power to the disciples. One often reads that this story is cast as a theophany—that is, a bold revelation of the divine; and anyone who turns to Job 9:8; Psalm 107:23-32; and Isaiah 41:4-10; 43:25 will see how deliberately John shaped his telling of this miracle to reflect and pick up the idea of the dramatic self-disclosure of God to humanity (see especially the parallels between this story and the Psalm). Moreover, John hints at the source of Jesus' amazing authority when he tells us that Jesus "withdrew again to the mountain by himself." Biblical tradition consistently associates the mountain with the presence and power of God. In contrast to Matthew who tells his reader that Jesus went off to pray, John says he went to the mountain "by himself," perhaps alluding to his identity.

The account of the events on the sea implicitly and explicitly contrasts the faith and power of Jesus with the lack of faith and lack of power of the disciples. The disciples are incapable of withstanding the chaotic forces of nature, and when Jesus comes to them they do not recognize him but fall back in fear. Jesus manifests the power of God and does what is humanly impossible; but the disciples cower in their own reasonable sense of inadequacy.

The story ends with Jesus having rescued the disciples and moved the boat to the other side of the sea. It is his person and presence that makes the miracle. His declaration, "It is I; do not be afraid," alludes to his identity and to the source of Christian security. "It is I" translates Greek words which served as the translation from Hebrew of the personal name of God, "I am." Thus, Jesus states his identity; and in his presence, the disciples are given the courage they do not otherwise have.

Proper 12: The Celebration

Classical homiletics distinguishes between three levels of meaning in dealing with a text, and no text is more suited to illustrate those levels than II Samuel 11:1. "In the spring of the

131

year, the time when kings go forth to battle . . . David remained at Jerusalem.''

The first level of meaning is that of the text itself, the literal level, or storytelling at its most basic. If the preacher were a sculptor and the text a block of marble, this form of preaching would consist of walking round and round the piece of marble and describing its contours, shades of color, and other physical characteristics. It would be an appreciation of the block of marble as a block of marble in its own right. Such a sermon succeeds to the degree that the preacher/storyteller brings the text to life in the imagination of the hearers. In his own way, Cecil B. DeMille did the same thing with his motion picture about this event in David's life. This kind of preaching is often thought of by congregants as "biblical," because they can easily relate it to the written text. One must ask, though, if the sculptor has completed her task when she has comprehended the block of marble. How does that make her any different from a geologist?

To pursue the analogy, the sculptor must move to a consideration of the potential that is in the marble, the possibility of a statue, and that leads to a second level of textual explication. This is the analogical or ethical level, an examination of possible moral implications latent in the story. Care should be taken to avoid a works-righteousness interpretation of the text, in this case on the lines of "the devil finds work for idle hands." If David had been doing his job, he wouldn't have had time for fooling around! Such judgments may not be wrong, but they may be relative to the context in which the passage is studied, so that the application in one setting may not be appropriate in another. The commentator above has focused on the issue of how we deal with power responsibly before God as at least one of the ethical dimensions of this text.

The third level of interpretation, the level of the finished statue, is the theological level. Here the preacher seeks out that which makes the text a word from God for her or his hearers. The first level may leave things as an interesting lesson in history or a literary exercise. The second level may be content with moral exhortation and encouragement. The third level is that which brings a shock of recognition as we see ourselves in the narrative. In this case, in the words of the commentator, we see ourselves as practical atheists (atheists in practice, not in belief) and so the foolish ones of the psalm. We are those who use the power or whatever else we have received from God in order to live as though God is not. This level supplements the second by stressing the divine source of our misused gifts and so we are called to judgment and forgiveness rather than attempts at self-betterment.

Notice that the concluding verses of the lesson from Ephesians are referred to in the commentary as a doxology and not as a benediction. These verses and the last two of the letter of Jude all too frequently appear as benedictions when in fact they do not pronounce a blessing upon the congregation, which is the function of benedictions (Latin, *benedicere*, meaning "to bless"). These are ascriptions of praise and more appropriately serve as conclusions to sermons.

The Gospel lesson today begins a month-long reading of John 6, where the major emphasis is on the bread of life motif. That suggests that the feeding of the five thousand rather than the stilling of the storm be the subject of the sermon unless in the Sundays to come the feeding narrative will be incorporated as part of its introduction. By reworking the Gospel lesson for last week, either the feeding or the storm narrative could be used then from Mark's version. Because the latter creates a break in the imagistic flow in John, it would be preferable to include Mark 6:45-51 as part of last week's reading and concentrate today on the feeding, omitting John 6:15-21. The content of the readings for the next five weeks suggests that the Lord's Supper would be a fitting way to begin and/or end this set of Sundays.

Proper Thirteen
Sunday Between July 31 and
August 6 Inclusive

Old Testament Texts

Second Samuel 11:26–12:13a describes how Nathan confronted David after he took Bathsheba and killed Uriah. Psalm 51:1-12 is a penitentiary prayer in which the guilt of the psalmist is confessed as a basis for petitioning God for deliverance.

The Lesson: *II Samuel 11:26–12:13*a

Reflecting on Evil

Setting. The tragedy of David-Bathsheba-Uriah acquired a central place in Israelite tradition. There are signs in the text which suggests that biblical writers came back several times to this event in order to reflect on the nature of human evil and divine atonement. In fact three levels of commentary may be woven into II Samuel 11–12. The first level of commentary comprises the narrative of II Samuel 11:2-27a and 12:15b-25. The first half of this story was the object of interpretation last week. Although this narrative is clearly negative in its evaluation of David, there is also a certain distance in the telling of the story. God is absent during the evil events in II Samuel 12:2-27a and then enters the story in 12:15b-25 by striking the child born to Bathsheba with disease until it eventually dies. In this story David pleads for the child, but it is of no avail. The Old Testament lesson for this week is a second level of commentary on the sin of David.

The Deuteronomistic writers of 11:27b–12:15a appear not to be satisfied with the dispassionate narrative that forms the subtext of the story. In view of this they provide additional commentary to probe further dimensions of David's evil action by introducing the prophetic figure, Nathan, who now confronts David with divine oracles. Yet even here scholars suspect two separate additions: the first being the parable and Nathan's accusation (11:27b–12:7a) with a theology of atonement at the close (12:13 15a, the guilt of David is transferred to the child); and the second being an extended litany contrasting God's graciousness and David's selfishness (12:7b-12). The tradition-historical development of II Samuel 11–12 underscores poignantly how Israel could not simply put the David-Bathsheba-Uriah tragedy behind them and get on with its national life. Instead, it remained an open wound, to which Israel was drawn back throughout its history. One could argue that the evil at the heart of this story is the turning point in the history of Israel for the Deuteronomistic writers, since it signals the beginning of the end for the Davidic monarchy in their extended history of Israel (Deuteronomy-Kings). The writers state this turning through the words of the prophet Nathan: "Thus says the LORD: I will raise up trouble against you from within your own house."

Structure. The brief overview of tradition history underscores how the boundaries of the lectionary text do not correspond exactly to the way in which the text developed. Starting the reading with 12:26, however, is probably preferred because it provides narrative setting for the confrontation between Nathan and David. Second Samuel 11:26–12:13a separates into the following two parts. Part 1 includes the introduction (11:26-12:1*a*), the presentation of a legal case to David in the form of a parable (12:1*b*-4), David's judgment on the case (12:5-6), and Nathan's application of the case to David (12:7*a*). Part 2 consists of oracles of threat in vv. 7*b*-10 and 11-12 (note the two instances of "Thus says the LORD" in v. 7*b* and 11), and it concludes with David's confession of guilt (v. 13*a*).

Significance. What is the nature of David's evil according to the Deuteronomistic writers? The parable provides the hermeneutical clue. Whether or not the parable was composed to provide commentary on David's sin or inserted into its present context is a matter of debate among scholars that need not be a primary concern for preaching. What is clear is that a series of contrasts within the parable are now meant to be a description of David and Uriah: rich and poor, much and little. In addition, a final contrast focuses directly on David alone: outward appearance and inward reality. When these contrasts are combined, they present the following message: The rich man not only stole the one precious possession of the poor man, but he gave the appearance of being generous to his guest. Thus the cruel theft is compounded by hypocrisy. The emphasis on hypocrisy is reinforced in v. 12 when God underscores how David's actions were meant to be private, and that God's punishment would be public. The truth of this statement is evident in the long tradition history of this text. Many generations, including ourselves, have reflected on David's private sin.

This text is difficult to preach if it is viewed statically as a morality play, because the point is so obvious. Another way to preach this text is to emphasize the progression in the character of David from blindness to recognition and finally confession. As inconceivable as it may appear to the reader, David is oblivious to the real point of the parable. And, only after the prophet Nathan hits him with a verbal two-by-four (v. 7, "You are the man!"), does David recognize himself in the story. This recognition is his salvation, and it leads to confession (v. 13, "I have sinned against the LORD."). The lectionary text ends at this point, and that is unfortunate because it gives the impression of a happy ending. David has apologized, and now we can go on to a new episode. Such a conclusion does not go to the heart of the evil that David has let loose with his actions, for an innocent child must die to atone for his guilt (v. 14, "Nevertheless, because by this deed you have utterly scorned the LORD, the child that is born to you shall die."), and, as we will see in the text for next week, David's kingdom will begin to collapse.

The Deuteronomistic writers underscore at least two points in their reflection on David's sin. The first is the nearly absurd blindness in David. Even the best humans, like David, have a gift for masking the real state of affairs to protect our own self-interest; to secure salvation we are required to recognize this flaw. And, second, evil has real consequences that cannot always be fixed even after we recognize it.

The Response: *Psalm 51:1-12*

Confessing Guilt

Setting. The prayer song or a petitionary prayer in Psalm 51 has also been pulled into the orbit of the David-Bathsheba-Uriah tragedy. Note how the historical commentary at the beginning of the psalm invites the reader to interpret the petition as coming from David after the prophet Nathan has unmasked his guilt in sleeping with Bethsheba and in killing her husband, Uriah, the Hittite. The historical setting underscores that the psalm is meant to be a liturgical guide of how we approach God at those times when we feel the most alienated.

Structure. Psalm 51:1-12 does not include the vow to praise that is central in vv. 13-19. Instead it focuses on the psalmist's confrontation of guilt and the plea for grace because of God's character. Psalm 51:1-12 separates into three parts: Verses 1-2 are a petition for mercy; vv. 3-5 are an acknowledgment of guilt; and, vv. 6-12 are a plea for deliverance.

Significance. Psalm 51:1-12 presents a powerful and

sustained confession of guilt that evolves into a plea for divine deliverance. When read in conjunction with II Samuel 11:26–12:13a, it functions as an expansion of David's short confession of guilt in v. 13a. As such the psalm probes the second point noted above that evil is not something that is easily fixed. The central motifs for conveying this fact are more hygienic than strictly ethical. In God's perspective, sin has reduced the psalmist to dirty laundry. Consequently, the psalmist confesses that sin is pollution or defilement from conception (v. 5), which God must wash (v. 2), cleanse (v. 2), and purge (v. 7) in order for it to be blotted out (v. 9). Such divine action is the content of God's steadfast love (v. 1).

New Testament Texts

The lessons continue to move through Ephesians and John 6. The text from Ephesians moves us into the second half of the epistle, while the reading from John 6 builds on elements of last week's lesson.

The Epistle: *Ephesians 4:1-16*

How Then Shall We Live?

Setting. As commentators regularly observe, Ephesians is the least situational of the thirteen letters attributed to Paul in the New Testament. Yet, the epistle shows a pronounced interest in practical matters. After chapters 1–3 make their elaborate, elevated, and elegant theological statement, chapters 4–6 take up the ordering of the everyday life of believers. The first section of the letter was punctuated with the doxology in 3:20-21. The second part of the epistle begins as did the outset of the letter with a personal reference and remarks from the apostle to the readers. The author shows an absolute conviction that theology finds its true importance in relation to the present experience of salvation in Christian living.

Structure. The sentences composing vv. 1-16 are highly

irregular in length. Verses 1-6 are a single sentence, as are v. 7, v. 8, v. 9, v. 10, and vv. 11-16. Thus, the entire lesson comprises two long, complex sentences, one at the beginning and one at the end—the opening statement is a call to unity and the closing comment explains that the different gifts Christ gives to believers are meant to work together for the collective good of the Church. Between these elaborate declarations are four short sentences, which work together to explain that the gifts of grace to individual believers are gifts from Christ himself. The overall pattern of thought here is movement from a call to unity to an explanation of diversity to an explanation of unity.

Significance. The call to Christian living is a call to unity of the fellowship of believers in love. We should understand that the love which unites the community of faith is God's own powerful love, for the call here to Christian unity in love is based ultimately on the singularity of God (see how the appeal peaks in v. 6). For the community of believers life together unified by love is nothing more or less than the experience of the peace of God's Spirit. Concretely, for those who are bonded together in peace by the power of God's love, there are discernible characteristics for life. The opening lines of this elaborate appeal for unity delineate certain prominent properties of Christian life. As we see the apostle urging the believers to a life worthy of their calling, we find a description of his manner of appeal: He calls to them in all humility, gentleness, patience, and forbearance (NRSV: "bearing with one another") in love—all of which are devoted to maintaining the unity of the Spirit. These are all fairly common biblical terms, and consulting scholarly commentaries, theological dictionaries, and use of a thorough concordance to do "word studies" of this vocabulary should provide much inspiration for proclamation.

The call to unity is justified in terms of the apparent creed in vv. 4-6 or 5-6. Notice the basis of Christian oneness: One body, one Spirit, one hope, one Lord, one faith, one baptism, one God. Theological systems that promote particularities or human distinctions that tend to divide the community of faith (and these days there are endless adjectival theologies!) are genuinely antithetical to the essence of God's will and essential Christian teaching. The tone of this passage will not, however, support a war of words on sub-Christian theological systems; rather, we find here a purely positive model for calling people to unity instead of calling them away from factionalism. Christianity is about oneness, because God is one! Let us say it over and over!

But Christian unity does not mean there are not differences or distinctions among the members of the community of faith. To deny differences is to deny the plain teaching of Scripture. Yet, we must come to see that whatever distinctions we recognize in terms of our talents, tendencies, and capacities are only legitimate when and because they work together to build up the community of faith. Our Lord Christ gives each of us whatever good gifts we possess with the express purpose that these gifts be used in concert with one another for harmony (not discord). A test of the legitimacy of a gift is whether it serves, or has the potential to serve, the whole community; if not, it may be a real talent or proclivity, but it is not a Christian gift. As Christians we are called to a unified life of love in the power of God's Spirit that means a profound experience of peace because we exercise the gracious gifts of Christ for the mutual benefit of the entire Church.

The Gospel: *John 6:24-35*

Jesus Christ, the Bread of Life

Setting. General remarks about the setting of our lesson for this week were offered in the discussion of the Gospel for Proper 12. Unlike the foregoing stories (feeding the five thousand and walking on the water) there is no parallel to the material in this lesson in the other Gospels.

Structure. Interpreters suggest a variety of structures for the verses of our lesson, but the dominant perspective seems to be as follows: (1) Verses 24-25 are part of a larger report in vv. 22-25 about the curiosity of the crowd on finding Jesus on the other side of the sea despite his not having access to a boat for crossing. The people finally put a question to Jesus. And (2) this query sets up the ensuing dialogue (vv. 26-34 or 35) which, in turn, will lead into the extensive "bread of life" discourse (vv. 35 or 36-59) which is not part of our lesson but which may help one grasp the sense of our lesson. Notice in the exchange between Jesus and the people in vv. 26-34 that Jesus confronts the people and makes revelatory declarations about himself rather than answers the question. In the discussion of significance we presuppose the crowd's curiosity and move to treat the dialogue (vv. 26-34) and Jesus' bold declaration (v. 35).

Significance. In the unconventional logic of the gospel according to John, the question of the crowd, which seems never to be answered, may mean far more than "How did you get across the lake?" Jesus certainly does not answer that simple question, but instead, he takes on the crowd and ends up making metaphorical, revelatory declarations about his true origin and identity.

The text is packed with significant terms and phrases—for example, "signs," "eternal life," "Son of Man," "[God's] seal," "the works of God," "believe," "sent," "the (true) bread from heaven," "comes down from heaven," and "life." These are uttered knowingly by Jesus and heard in seeming ignorance by those with whom he speaks. The text works with a common Johannine literary technique, wherein the conversation possesses two levels of meaning. Jesus talks in metaphors about divine truths and wonders, but the people hear and think in earth-bound terms that preclude their understanding. As readers of this Gospel we stand in a privileged position between Jesus and the people, knowing far less than Jesus who teaches us, but far more than the people who never seem to have a clue about their ignorance or Jesus' meanings.

As an inventory of the terminology in these verses reveals, this passage, like most others in John, contains the whole gospel in a nutshell. If we will allow ourselves to stand with the people, but with the capacity to hear and understand Jesus, then this lesson imparts a profound message indeed.

Like the people we wonder about Jesus, Who is he? Where did he come from? What is he doing here? As he replies in his strange Johannine voice he tells us these things and more. We have a tendency to come to Jesus for the wrong reasons, most often to get something from him that is far less than he is prepared and willing to give. In our small-mindedness we thwart the riches of God's grace. Our limited perspective gives us little expectations. We give our lives to achieving ends that are temporal, ephemeral; perhaps seeking the good, we never come to know the better and the best. Or, if we know the better (Moses' manna), we may be so content with it that we never experience the exhilarating freedom of faith in Christ.

Jesus Christ comes to us as the grace of God, calling us beyond our limited perspective and out of our limited patterns of living. God's gift to us is a transforming relationship to Jesus Christ who empowers us to live into a fullness of life that is God's real intention for our living. If we can come through our encounter with this text to the point that we simply raise our level of expectations, then we have heard what the passage is saying in these verses. The text simply provokes greater expectations. Other crucial questions will naturally follow from perceiving the basic point that in Jesus Christ God is calling us beyond the current limits of our living to a new and vital life oriented toward "eternal life" and "the works of God." Naturally, we wonder what such a life looks like; but the scope of our lesson in the context of the series of texts from John 6 may require us to put this kind of question on hold, for we learn in another passage, not this one, what it means never to hunger or thirst through our belief in Jesus Christ.

Proper 13: The Celebration

The epistle and Gospel lessons provide for the observance of baptism and the Eucharist respectively as sign-acts helping to interpret some portion of the Scriptures read in the service. A hymn that relates well to both events and to the epistle particularly is E. H. Plumptre's, "Thy Hand, O God, Hath Guided." It is not easily found in American hymnals, so selected stanzas are printed below from a contemporary revision by Laurence Hull Stookey. The full text of both the original and the revision can be found in Dr. Stookey's book, *Baptism: Christ's Act in the Church* (Nashville: Abingdon Press, 1982), pp. 196-97. Aurelia and Lancashire are suggested tunes.

> Your hand, O God, has guided
> your flock from age to age;
> the wondrous tale is written
> full clear on every page;
> our forebears owned your goodness
> and we their deeds record;
> and both of this bear witness,
> one church, one faith, one Lord

> Your heralds brought glad tidings
> to greatest and to least;
> they bade each rise and hasten
> to share Christ's holy feast;
> and this was all their teaching,
> in every deed and word,
> to all alike proclaiming
> one church, one faith, one Lord.

> Your mercy will not fail us,
> nor leave your work undone;
> with your right hand to help us,
> the victory shall be won.
> By those on earth and angels
> your name shall be adored,

and this shall be their anthem:
one church, one faith, one Lord.

If the Epistle lesson is used as the occasion for preaching about how our ministry is based in our baptism, and how our ministries vary according to the gifts the Spirit has given us, then the following prayer may be used either as the opening prayer or during the intercessions.

Almighty and everlasting God, by whose Spirit the whole body of your faithful people is governed and sanctified: Receive our supplications and prayers which we offer before you for all members of your holy Church, that in their vocation and ministry they may truly and devoutly serve you; through our Lord and Savior Jesus Christ.

If today's psalm is not used as a response to the Old Testament lesson, it may serve as a responsive prayer of confession or be rewritten to make a shorter unison prayer. After it has been prayed, and before the declaration of pardon or words of the assurance, the following little-used stanza from "Rock of Ages" might be used. It picks up on the themes of pollution and washing mentioned in the commentary.

Nothing in my hand I bring,
simply to thy cross I cling;
naked, come to thee from dress;
helpless, look to thee for grace;
foul, I to the fountain fly;
wash me, Savior, or I die.

Proper Fourteen
Sunday Between
August 7 and 13 Inclusive

Old Testament Texts

Second Samuel 18 is the account of Absalom's death. Psalm 130 is a pentitential prayer.

The Lesson: *II Samuel 18:5-9, 15, 31-33*

A Story in Which Everything Is Wrong

Setting. The drama, which concludes with the execution of Absalom, reaches all the way back to II Samuel 13 and extends forward into II Samuel 19. It begins with an incestuous rape. Amnon (the eldest son of David) lures Tamar (one of David's daughters and the sister of Absalom) into his bedroom under the pretext of being sick. After she enters he rapes her and discards her like a day-old newspaper. David hears about it but does nothing, while Absalom consoles Tamar and two years later kills Amnon, before he flees to the city of Geshur, where he remains for three years (II Samuel 13). Joab enters the story in chapter 14 by hiring the wise woman from Tekoa to present a judgment to David about a conflict in her family, which is really a thinly disguised synopsis of David's own troubled family. As in the case with Nathan, David lacks any insight into the analogy until the woman explicitly makes the point: Why not forgive Absalom and allow him to return to Jerusalem? He does, and Absalom lives in Jerusalem for two years (II Samuel 14). Once in Jerusalem Absalom undercuts David's judicial authority by turning people away at the city gate (which is the equivalent of contemporary law courts). This activity goes on for four years, until Absalom requests that he be allowed to sacrifice at Hebron, which David allows. Once in Hebron Absalom claims kingship, forcing David to flee Jerusalem (II Samuel 15). The revolt continues through II Samuel 16 17. The lectionary text includes scenes from the final confrontation.

Structure. The lectionary text highlights David's ambivalence and grief about the conflict with Absalom. Verses 5-9 include David's request that Absalom be dealt with gently. Verse 15 is an account of Absalom's death. Verses 31-33 close with a snapshot of David weeping over the loss of his son.

Significance. This is a difficult text to preach because proper interpretation requires knowledge of the larger context. If the death of Absalom is read in isolation, David's grief becomes overstated, and we begin to psychologize the story too much by thinking how terrible he must feel, which is usually then connected by the preacher to how terrible we would feel. Clearly he does feel terrible, and his grief is important to the story, but it is not the purpose of the story in this context. The entire narrative of II Samuel 13–18 must be read in light of the tragedy that swallows David, Bathsheba, and Uriah. The evil of that event is still working itself out as the prophet Nathan predicted: "I will raise up trouble for you within your own house" (II Samuel 12:11), which means that David is both a victim and an agent of this evil.

Second Samuel 13–18 is an extended story in which everything is wrong. Central to the story is David's inability to mediate justice. He does not address the rape of Tamar when he is told about it (II Samuel 13:21). For a second time he is presented as lacking insight into his own actions and situation when the wise woman from Tekoa holds a mirror to his face with her thinly disguised family problem (II Samuel 14:1-20; compare also the parable of Nathan in II Samuel 12). David does not appear to be administrating justice at the city gate as was required of the king (II Samuel 15:1-6). And he is unable to pursue justice during the revolt of Absalom. While people are risking their lives to preserve his rule, David requests that they deal gently with his son (II Samuel 18:5).

David is presented throughout these chapters as a character who has replaced justice with a sentimentality that is limited to his own family. The careful logging of chronology throughout the story underscores how David's actions (or lack of them) are not simply isolated occurrences. Instead, they represent a pattern of behavior that spans eleven years. Furthermore few other central characters emerge as heroes. Amnon is scum. Absalom starts off heroically by taking in Tamar, but his actions degenerate into self-interest. Joab lacks any ideals and instead functions as an efficient bureaucrat who has no time for moral reflection (II Samuel 18:14). The heroes of this story are those who supported David by risking their lives against all odds. But as the narrative makes clear in II Samuel 19, those who should have been treated as heroes in the end must creep into the city as though they were cowards, because when the battle is over David is unable to rise above his own wallowing sentimentality. In the end David stays in power, but everybody is dirty.

The fall of David was rooted in sexual abuse and murder. He stole Bathsheba and had Joab kill Uriah because it was the most efficient thing to do under the circumstances. Second Samuel 13–19 plays out this same drama in David's family. It, too, begins with sexual abuse, and it ends with Joab executing Absalom because it was the most efficient thing to do under the circumstances. There is nothing redeeming in the development of the narrative, and the outer boundaries of the unit underscore this point by the way in which the motif of shame is applied to the innocent victims. Shame is defined as a situation in which the opposite of what was intended in fact happens (for further discussion of shame see the First Sunday in Lent in Year A). The narrative opens with Tamar in a situation of shame because of the rape and rejection of her brother (II Samuel 13:13), and it ends with David's troops in a situation of shame because of David's confusion which has resulted in his loving those who hate him and hating those who love him (II Samual 19:5-6). The revolt of Absalom is a story about mixed motives which in the end are evil.

The Response: *Psalm 130*

A Penitential Prayer

Setting. The penitential prayer of Psalm 130 provides the liturgical language of how we petition for God's grace when we become aware of our shame. This is a powerful psalm. The setting of the psalm is ambiguous. Yet two things are clear. First, the psalmist is at a great distance from God. And, second, the speaker is painfully self-conscious of just how alienated he or she is from God. Thus there is a desperate quality to the opening petitions.

Structure. Psalm 130:1-3 moves quickly through a cry for help (vv. 1-2), a confession of sin (v. 3). The remainder of the psalm moves out of the realization of God's grace in v. 4 and begins to explore hope, both for the psalmist (vv. 5-6) and for the community of faith (vv. 7-8), because God is gracious (vv. 5-8).

Significance. Psalm 130:1-3 is an excellent counterpart to the narrative about Absalom's revolt, because it provides liturgical language of hope in situations where human motive is at best mixed and everything appears to go wrong. The opening cry for help in vv. 1-2 underscores how distant God is, while the confession of sin in v. 3 underscores how the consequences of sin go far beyond what any human action could do to improve the situation. These insights bring the psalmist to the ultimate truth that in the end only God can undo our alienation in a broken world—only God can forgive sin. This revelation is the turning point in the psalm, which provides the basis for the soliloquy on hope in vv. 5-8. Psalm 130 goes far beyond the narrative situation of II Samuel 13–19, because it is unclear at the end of this story whether David's cry acquires the focus on God that is evident in the psalm.

New Testament Texts

The lessons continue the sequential readings from the practical portion of Ephesians and the "bread of life" discourse in John 6. The advice in Ephesians becomes eminently tenable, and Jesus' speech in John 6 takes on a new polemical edge as he reiterates and amplifies his declarations about his identity and purposes.

The Epistle: *Ephesians 4:25–5:2*

The Practical Side of Imitating God

Setting. At v. 25 of Ephesians 4 the epistle takes a hard turn into explicit parenesis—that is, plain practical instruction. The earlier portion of the second part of the letter (4:1-24) issued a call to unity (vv. 1-16) and contrasted the readers' former manner of life with their current Christian living (vv. 17-24). While these sections of the epistle were concerned with everyday life, they were more the rationale than the routine of Christian life.

Structure. Our lesson is actually a distinguishable unit of material within the epistle precisely because it is composed of a series of eight nearly independent statements that are made in no particular order. Only 4:26-27 and 5:1-2 are sentences of more than one verse. The beginning of the series is discernible because of the rhetorical opening, "So then . . ." which actually starts to unpack the principle articulated in 4:24, "clothe yourselves with the new self, created according to the likeness of God in true righteousness and holiness.'' Similarly, the series comes to a close in 5:1-2 which begins, ''Therefore be imitators of God. . . .'' From this frame we may infer that the collection of statements from 4:25-32 is dealing with the reality of what believers do in imitation of God.

Significance. The verses of our lesson advise us about things to do and things not to do as we live imitating God as God's children. Things to do in imitation of God include (1) speaking the truth; (2) being angry without sinning; (3) laboring and working honestly; (4) sharing with the needy; (5) saying what is useful for building up and so giving grace to those who hear; (6) being kind to one another; (7) forgiving one another; and (8) living in love. Things not to do include (1) lying; (2) letting the sun set on our anger; (3) making room for the devil; (4) stealing; (5) engaging in evil talk; (6) grieving the Holy Spirit; and (7) being bitter, wrathful, angry, quarrelsome, slanderous, and malicious.

Most of this advice is straightforward and easily understood. But perhaps a word is appropriate on the advice in 4:30. This is one of the glimmers of future eschatology in the entire letter. The mention of the Christians being sealed with the Holy Spirit for the day of redemption is a metaphor about current life in relation to the day of final judgment. The image may be related to the Passover, but in any case the idea is this: We are not to live in the present in a manner inconsistent with the future life we will lead when God's final judgment is enacted. Our lives in the present are to be accurate anticipations of the realization of the will of God in the end. The Spirit claims us now for the future, so that our present life is defined in relation to and in terms of God's future.

One other set of items is noteworthy. Christians are called to be imitators of God. We are not, however, simply told to be good and left guessing what that means. God's Spirit grasps our lives, and in the presence and the power of God, by God's very power, we are able to live as true children of God. Moreover, God has shown us who he is and what it means to be like God. ''God in

Christ has forgiven [us]," and we are called to "live in love, as Christ loved us and gave himself for us." In Christ God steps forth into this world, into our lives, and we see God. God tells us what he's come for—to redeem us. To do for us what we cannot—even with all the self-helps in the world—do for ourselves. God has come to forgive us. God has come to make us new.

The Gospel: *John 6:35, 41-51*

Bread and Belief That Mean Eternal Life

Setting. Having fed the five thousand, walked on the water, and begun to converse with the crowds using the metaphors "bread of life" and "bread of heaven" to declare his identity, Jesus continues to speak. The crowd continues to listen and respond. The speech is highly repetitive in vocabulary and thought. Yet we find a remarkable new turn in the verses of our lesson, for now the members of the crowd who are shocked by Jesus' words and resistant to his teaching are identified as "the Jews." In John's Gospel this designation is applied to Jesus' archenemies. This is striking because Jesus himself, all his disciples, and those among whom he works (many of whom believe) are all Jews. This language points to John's own time, when he and the other Christian members of his community have been thrown out of the synagogue by "the Jews." With spectacles ground in his own day, John takes the readers of the Gospel back to Jesus' time and reviews the events of that earlier day through the lens of the later Christian community's time.

Structure. The opening line of the lesson has Jesus repeat his initial pronouncement, "I am the bread of life," from the previous portion of the "bread of life" discourse. This statement sets up the story unit in vv. 41-51. There we find that "the Jews" murmur against Jesus, discounting his declaration by claiming that they know his true origin which they state in purely human terms. In response Jesus speaks again, first clarifying their failure to believe and, then, restating his identity and explaining what exactly that means in relation to the work of God in relation to humanity. In simple form the passage has four parts or movements, which may suggest the shape of a sermon: (1) Jesus is the bread of life. (2) People find that hard to swallow (pun intended!). (3) The capacity to believe in Jesus Christ is not a purely human effort, it is a divine work. (Some people will find this hard to swallow, too—no pun.) (4) Nevertheless, belief in Jesus Christ gives "eternal life." There are other striking subthemes woven into this outline—for example, Jesus' unique knowledge of the Father; and these may be treated accordingly in developing the various elements of the sermon and worship.

Significance. Jesus "talks funny" in the Fourth Gospel. Sometimes it's his images, and sometimes it's the meaning of what he says, but many times he's hard to hear. In our lesson he tells us, "I am the bread of life" and "I have come down from heaven." Thus we have one puzzling image and one puzzling statement, both of which leave us wondering more than a little bit. In one way, what Jesus says is plain: He is talking about his divine identity. But even seeing that causes questions, for we humans simply cannot comprehend what it means to be divine. We know that to be divine is to be different—different from being human; but since we are not divine, it's hard to know what the difference is! But when Jesus says he is the heavenly bread of life, he gives us plenty of clues. Bread is something we eat. It nourishes us. It sustains us. And at points in our lives it even makes us grow. Maybe that's who Jesus is, God come to us to nourish us, to sustain us, and to make us grow. Moreover, maybe like bread, Jesus has to be consumed to do us any good!

But not surprisingly, some people have a hard time with this Jesus. Beyond the enigmatic images and cryptic sayings, all of us know of a Jesus who was plenty human. He lived a human life—from a humble birth to a nasty death. Sometimes we think about his words and deeds, and Jesus is impressive; but when we think about the beating he took and the way he died, he doesn't cut a very impressive figure: nail-cut, head cocked back, crying out for a drink, bleeding, he died. A human among humans he lived, and a human among humans he died. And so, when we hear him saying, "I am this-or-that" and "I came down from heaven," many of us wonder. In this world it's hard to get away from simple, honest doubts.

Yet, as we listen we hear another strange message in Jesus' talking. He says that the ability to believe in him is not at all a human achievement. How does he put it? "No one can come to me unless drawn by the Father who sent me. . . . It is written in the prophets, 'And they shall all be taught by God' " (vv. 41, 42). If Jesus is hard to swallow, this kind of thinking about God is equally as hard to take. What kind of God is this who draws people to Jesus Christ? What kind of God sends down his Son to live and work among humans before being brutally put to death? What kind of God offers his Son as the bread of heaven so that the world may have life? The gospel says this is a God of grace and glory, a God of love and life. And our lesson tells us that the God of grace, glory, love, and life works among us humans to draw us to Jesus Christ, so that in relation to him we may truly live.

The capacity to believe in Jesus Christ is God's gift of faith. The good news is that as we come to Christ, drawn by God, we are given eternal life. "Eternal life" is John's code for naming a transformed quality of life that has its very real beginnings in this world and that is so qualitatively different from our normal mode of living that it cannot be exhausted in this life. The quality and quantity of eternal life are essentially infinite, because eternal life is the life of God rooted in us as we are rooted in God through our belief in Jesus Christ.

Proper 14: The Celebration

The reference to the seal of the Holy Spirit in the epistle lesson may refer liturgically to the combined action of baptism and anointing with oil. Either or both together are often referred to as "the sealing" in the ancient writings of the Church. When

153

confirmation became distinct from baptism in the West, the baptismal anointing either dropped out altogether or its significance diminished by the insistence that confirmation was the "completion of baptism." The matter is still being vigorously discussed in the churches. Today's lesson may lead to a consideration of the meaning of baptism and confirmation in the sermon, or the celebration of those rites, or both.

How seriously we take the seal of baptism is an important question to deal with. Do we believe that we are "marked for life" by that event because of God's faithfulness to us? In the ancient world the seal was an identifying mark or a sign of ownership. When Paul speaks of Christians being sealed by the Holy Spirit he is saying that they are marked, set apart for life through the gift of the Spirit. To be sealed in this way was to be made like Christ, because the Father had also set his seal on him (see John 6:27 in last week's Gospel lesson). In baptism we are "signed, sealed, and delivered," quite literally. Irenaeus uses the image of sealing or "stamping" in an interesting way:

> Even as the Lord commits to the Holy Ghost that man of his, who had fallen among thieves; whom he did himself pity, and bound up his wounds, giving two royal pennies, that we receiving by the Spirit the image and inscription of the Father and the Son, might cause the penny entrusted to us to bear fruit, accounting for it to the Lord with manifold increase. (J. Keble, trans., *Five Books of St. Ireneus, Bishop of Lyons, Against Heresies* [Oxford: James Parker, 1872], p. 274)

This interpretation of what the Lord did for the man fallen among thieves is worth noting. Nothing in Luke justifies saying that the Lord "commits him to the Holy Spirit," unless he is making a connection with the phrase "pouring on oil" in the description of how the Samaritan cared for the injured man (Luke 10:34). Is Irenaeus thinking of ritual action he has seen performed at baptisms? It is also interesting to note that he speaks of the "royal" pennies having an image and inscription (see the story of paying taxes to Caesar), which is imparted to

Christians as their obverse and reverse sides. This stamping would make more sense if Irenaeus were referring to some ritual action known to himself.

Paul's exhortation today to the Ephesians is interesting because it suggests that the image imprinted by the Spirit remains even when we devalue ourselves by the way in which we live. It might be to the credit of the congregation that the thieves went to church because they at least knew they belonged there; they belonged to Christ. It may be at this point that American middle-class churches have the most difficult time understanding the radical character of the gospel. We so often give the impression that even though grace is free and unmerited, it is only available to those who don't need it. A colleague tells of visiting an inner-city Roman Catholic church where the priest, in his sermon, chastised the young men there for taking guns to school during the week. My friend observed that the church must have been doing something right since the gun toters were there to be chastised. Might the answer have to do with ecclesiology at its most profound, at its understanding of how radically baptism makes us a part of Christ, brands us so deeply that no surgery on our part will remove all the traces?

The following Isaac Watts hymn relates well the emphases of both New Testament lessons. Use a short meter tune such as St. Thomas or Boylston.

> Jesus invites his saints
> to meet around his board;
> here pardoned sinners sit, and hold
> communion with their Lord.
>
> For food he gives his flesh,
> he bids us drink his blood;
> amazing favor, matchless grace
> of our descending God!
>
> This holy bread and wine
> maintains our fainting breath,

155

by union with our living Lord,
and interest in his death.

Our heavenly Father calls
Christ and his members one;
we the young children of his love,
and he the first-born Son.

We are but several parts
of this same broken bread;
our body has its several limbs,
but Jesus is the Head.

Let all our powers be joined
his glorious name to raise;
pleasure and love fill every mind,
and every voice be praise.

Proper Fifteen
Sunday Between
August 14 and 20 Inclusive

Old Testament Texts

I Kings 2:10-12; 3:3-14 is the story of how God granted Solomon wisdom and Psalm 111 is a hymn of praise.

The Lesson: *I Kings 2:10-12; 3:3-14*

An Ideal Ruler

Setting. The central portion of the lectionary text consists of a dream theophany to Solomon at the outset of his reign. The setting of the story is Gibeon, not Jerusalem, where the new king has gone to sacrifice. This fact causes some tension in the present form of the text. One of the principle beliefs of the Deuteronomistic editors (those responsible for writing Deuteronomy-Kings) was that worship should only take place at one central location. Note the comment in v. 3 that even though Solomon loved God and walked in the same path as his father, David, his flaw was sacrificing at high places other than Jerusalem. The centralization of worship in Jerusalem, however, was not a central tenant of Israelite belief at the time of Solomon, and scholars have speculated that his trip to Gibeon may very well have been for the purpose of the dream theophany that still occupies the central place in the story. The text may in fact reflect a pattern of ritual incubation in the ancient Near East, in which kings sought revelation, while also seeking to be channels of divine blessing for their kingdoms. See other commentaries for possible parallels in Canaanite, Egyptian, and other Mesopotamian literature.

Structure. The lectionary text includes, as an introduction, the death notice of David and the establishment of Solomon as king in I Kings 2:10-12. The closing line of this introduction, that Solomon's kingdom was "firmly established" (Hebrew, *kun*), may be somewhat deceiving because the remainder of the chapter describes how he first killed his elder brother Adonijah, then banished the priest Abiathar to Anathoth, before also killing Joab and Shimei. After these events the text comes full circle in 2:46 by summarizing how the kingdom was "firmly established" (Hebrew, *kun*) by Solomon. These events, along with a notice about Solomon's marriage to Pharaoh's daughter (3:1-3) provide the background for the dream theophany at Gibeon. I Kings 3:3-14 separates into three parts. Verses 3-5 serve as an introduction in three ways: by providing positive commentary on Solomon (v. 3), by establishing the cultic setting of the story at Gibeon (v. 4), and by introducing the dream theophany with the divine offer to grant Solomon a wish (v. 5). Verses 6-9 consist of Solomon's two-part response: first, he reviews God's activity with David (v. 6); and then requests wisdom because of the difficulty of ruling so many people (vv. 7-9). Verses 10-14 are an extended divine speech, which underscores how unusual Solomon's request for wisdom was by first listing the more expected requests and then by praising the choice of wisdom. Although v. 15 is not part of the lectionary text, it brings the story full circle by describing Solomon awakening from a dream and then making offerings to God—this time at Jerusalem rather than Gibeon.

Significance. The theophany in I Kings 3:3-14 paints an ideal picture of how power should be exercised. Several aspects of the speech underscore the ideal character of the story. The first is the dream setting at a central cultic site. For a moment the king and the reader are removed from the issues of realpolitik that have dominated I Kings 2 (for example, political executions and exile) and, in a dream state, are encouraged to reflect on the exercise of power without the preoccupation of losing it. Second, the divine speech in vv. 10-14 provides the moral commentary. Here the reader learns that power is not meant to be exercised for self-preservation (long life), self-aggrandizement (wealth), or vindictive purposes (death of enemies). The third, and central feature that accentuates the ideal, is Solomon's actual request for wisdom. For a brief moment in a dream he acknowledges his lack of insight ("I do not know how to go out or come in.") and the overwhelming responsibility that accompanies the acquisition of power ("a great people, so numerous they cannot be numbered or counted"). The clarity of this moment gives rise to the request for understanding.

Language within the text prompts associations with other motifs throughout the Old Testament that further accentuate the ideal character of this text. The two primary promises that run throughout the Old Testament—that Israel would one day be a great nation and have a land (see, for example, Genesis 12:1-4)—are both fulfilled in this text. Solomon repeats the language of one part of this promise when he describes Israel as being a great people, while his position as king is a fulfillment of the other. The text underscores how after the divine promises of salvation are fulfilled, the central issue for the people of God becomes the acquisition of wisdom and its use in shaping how power is used. Note how wisdom language dominates the text: *understanding mind* (v. 9, 11), *discernment* (vv. 9, 11, 12), and *wise* (v. 12). Such language invites comparison to Isaiah 11:3 where the ideal messianic king is also described as someone who is wise because he does not "decide by what his ears hear."

The larger setting of the story provides a caution on how we reflect on the ideal. Many of the issues within Solomon's dream theophany contrast sharply with his activities in II Kings 2. The dream setting at a cultic site contrasts to the issues of realpolitik that dominate the political purges in II Kings 2. Then, too, the divine speech in vv. 10-14 could be read as providing condemnation of Solomon, who, before he had hardly seized power, was already using it for self-preservation and vindictive purposes through his political executions. For a moment in a dream we are given a glimpse of the ideal way in which power must be exercised among the people of God. Such ideal power is elusive and in the end a fragile divine gift. By locating this ideal use of power in a real person the Deuteronomistic writers are stating that the exercise of divine wisdom is possible for the people of God. The setting of a dream, and the larger context of ruthless political pragmatism, however, suggests that the ideal is not easy to attain. The odd conclusion of this episode in 3:15*a* catches the ambiguity of the text in its larger context: "Then Solomon awoke; it had been a dream." Was it real? Only the exercise of his power will answer the question.

The Response: *Psalm 111*

Celebrating the Reliability of God

Setting. Psalm 111 is a hymn of praise in an acrostic form. An acrostic psalm occurs when every line begins with a letter of the Hebrew alphabet so that by the end the reader has gone through the Hebrew equivalent of the English ABC's. Psalms 111 and 112 are both acrostic in form and may very well be related to each other. As you may imagine, the requirement of the acrostic form does not allow for a great deal of thematic development. Instead we are given a smorgasbord of praise to God.

Structure. Psalm 111 follows the general three-part form of a hymn: an introductory summons to praise, reasons why God should be praised, and a conclusion. The summons to praise occurs in the opening verse, where the singer of the psalm declares that God will now be praised in the setting of the worshiping community. The reasons for praise are listed in vv. 2-9. Most of the reasons for praise in Psalm 111 focus on the works of God—that is, his acts of salvation. The psalm ends in v. 10 with a didactic conclusion that picks up the focus of v. 2, which inaugurated the reasons for praise. Thus the great works of God that we are encouraged to study in v. 2, and which are then listed in vv. 3-9, are the beginning of wisdom for humans who live out the salvation of God (v. 10).

Significance. The central point of Psalm 111 when it is read in combination with I Kings 2:10-12; 3:3-14 is the emphasis on wisdom at the conclusion of the psalm in v. 10. The psalmist introduces a motif that has been absent from the Old Testament lesson when stating how "the fear of the Lord is the beginning of wisdom." Where the psalm connects more firmly with the Old Testament text is in the next line where wisdom becomes a matter of practice rather than theory. The practice of wisdom, the psalmist states, is in fact "good understanding." This is the same point that was made at the conclusion to the dream theophany. Wisdom is real when we see it in practice.

New Testament Texts

Our lesson from Ephesians takes us another step along the way of practical advice for the life of faith. The text from John 6 takes up still another segment of Jesus' elaborate "bread of life" discourse. Little unites these texts other than their shared central conviction that genuine Christian living is absolutely related to Jesus Christ.

The Epistle: *Ephesians 5:15-20*

The Dimensions of Truly Wise Living

Setting. Having struck an eschatological note in the last part of chapter 4, the author uses a dualistic contrast between light and darkness in the first half of chapter 5 to ground his admonition to live a Christian life rather than one of debauchery. In the next basic section, the verses of our lesson, the author continues his line of thought; but now he shifts to a contrast between wisdom and foolishness.

Structure. The basic outline of the argument is set in vv. 15-17:

Christians are to lead lives of wisdom, not foolishness; the rationale given for exhortation to wise living echoes the earlier eschatological note (4:30), saying, "Be careful then . . . making the most of the time, because the days are evil." Verse 18, then, issues a very concrete warning and a specific, if more nebulous, admonition that is filled out in concrete terms in vv. 19-20. In essence the passage is this: In light of the time live wisely; stay sober and filled with the Spirit—which means worship and thanksgiving.

Significance. The lesson advocates wise living for believers. In one way the lines of the passage are forthright, but in another way they are very subtle. It is easy to read this text and actually miss much of what the author is saying in advocating a careful life of wisdom. This word of encouragement is more than a call to decency and common sense, although the author would certainly find a place for upstanding and sensible conduct. Yet, the author does offer a distinctively Christian definition of wise living.

Wise living has perspective. The author calls for the readers to be aware of the time. This remark is not overtly eschatological, but read in the context of the entire letter, and remembering that the letter comes from the context of early Christianity, it is safe to understand the author's words in some relation to eschatology. The author recognizes that our lives are being lived in a context of special urgency. Time is not an absolute, rather it is qualified by the authority of God who stands over time. In and through Jesus Christ, God exercises judgment over the quality of human life lived in worldly time. One thing that makes time especially perilous is that we are always tempted to live as if there is no tomorrow—namely, for the self in the now. But in fact we are called to live with a constant concern for God's priorities, which do and will ultimately determine whether we have made the most of the time.

Wise living takes its cue from divine volition. Wise living is established by discerning and doing the will of God. In a community of religious faith the capacity for comprehending

God's will is facilitated in a variety of ways. We have history, tradition, Scripture, reason, and experience to name a few aids for grasping God's will and guiding our lives. But perhaps the greatest asset we have for wise living is the third item the author names, which qualifies the wise living of believers.

Wise living is done in the presence and the power of the Spirit of God. Early Christianity was genuinely charismatic. Believers lived with a profound conviction that God was really present and constantly at work among them through the Holy Spirit. God's Spirit opened wise mouths, gave wise hearts, granted intestinal fortitude, and sustained "body" energy for the faithful living of genuinely godly lives. Thus, through the Spirit believers are able to live in the thankfulness of praise with lives oriented toward the same God who gave the Spirit as a gift to enable wise living.

Finally, the author informs us that wise living has a personal dimension about it that transcends merely formal religion and merely moral existence. The wise life is lived in the name of our Lord Jesus Christ. The ability to name the divine in intimate terms, because God has actually been revealed to us in the person of Jesus Christ, gives us a relationship with God through Jesus Christ, which actually means that we live our lives under the lordship of Christ. God's time, God's will, and God's Spirit can be as real, or more real to us than we are to ourselves, because these matters are personal in Jesus Christ. We live wisely as Christians through a relationship with Jesus Christ, who—more than abstract notions of the divine and more than the formal requirements of a moral system—is ours as friend and family in all dimensions of life.

The Gospel: *John 6:51-58*

The Key to Being Alive

Setting. Pastors who have preached from the passages out of the "bread of life" discourse over the course of the past three weeks and who are either brave or foolish enough to attempt to do so again this week deserve all the help they can get. The lectionary has us in an extremely repetitive section of the gospel according to John, wherein Jesus speaks over and over about himself as the heavenly bread of life. Remarkably, however, as similar as these passages are week after week, there are essential differences in the texts that make each, despite its redundancy, somewhat unique.

Structure. From the initial "I am" statement to the end of the text, the lesson has a patterned, discernible structure of five pairs of remarks:

1. Declaration (51*a*) + Declaration (51*b*)
2. Difficulty (52) + Declaration (53)
3. Declaration (54) + Explanation (55)
4. Declaration (56) + Explanation (57)
5. Explanation (58*a*) + Declaration (58*b*)

The mood of declaration dominates, although there is an effort to provide explanation(s) for the emphatic but enigmatic statements—which, even in the course of the passage, cause genuine difficulties for comprehension. The shape and substance of this lesson are, as usual, suggestive for preaching.

Significance. Jesus himself unpacks the meaning of his loaded phrase, "I am the bread of life that came down from heaven." We have seen that statement alone puzzle the characters in John's narrative, but now Jesus fills out his statement and seems to cause equal or greater uncertainty. Jesus is heavenly bread and whoever eats that bread, which is his flesh, will live forever. This means that Jesus' own person, especially in relation to his death (*flesh* is an allusion), is charged with the capacity to grant eternal life.

Seeing this much of the sense of Jesus' statement is some progress, but "the Jews" in the story should provide us with comfort, for as this story has it, even Jesus' original hearers did not fully comprehend what he was saying. Again, the problem of understanding is that the characters in this story are thinking on two levels. "The Jews" are literalists, and while there is a plain sense to what Jesus says, he still speaks with a heavenly tone that strikes human ears with uncommon and unintelligible sounds. And so, Jesus speaks further, returning to his declarative mode. The first level of declaration was practically a promise ("whoever eats . . . will live forever"), but now the tone becomes almost threatening ("unless you eat . . . you have no life in you"). Here, we move to the level of faith claims or even revelation. Jesus asserts that his person and saving death (the reference to the saving quality of Jesus' death become explicit with the inclusion of "blood") are indispensable for well-being and salvation. What kind of hermeneutic can we apply to this statement?

Rather than explain directly, we find Jesus making another declaration that moves back to the level of promise ("Those who eat . . . have eternal life . . . I will raise them up"). Jesus' power to give life is clarified in part as his capacity to overcome death by resurrection, and the whole passage takes on an eschatological cast with the mention of "on the last day." The power Jesus speaks of is God's own power, to raise the dead in the context of final judgment; and Jesus explains himself by saying his flesh is "true food" and his blood is "true drink." True as opposed to what? Recall that Jesus came in the Fourth Gospel speaking the truth to achieve salvation for humans who were in darkness. Truth is a category of divine power for John, and Jesus speaks the truth by everything he says and does as the incarnate Word of God. Jesus' identity in relation to God makes him true and is his power. But still, even when we see this much of the sense of Jesus' statements, do we fully understand?

Fortunately, Jesus continues to speak, returning to his declarative mode. He talks now in categories of relationship (as was implied in the use of *true* in the previous statement). Because God is alive, a living God, and because Jesus was sent by God the Father as God's Son, Jesus lives by the very power of God alive in him. In relation to humans, Jesus is the presence of the living God, and through their relationship to him ("abide in me") humans are personally related to God who is the living Father, the God of life, who extends life to the world in Jesus Christ.

The lesson ends with still another word of explanation, which leads to a final declaration. Believers have life because in Jesus Christ they experience a dynamic dimension of the power of God that goes beyond previous experiences of God. Our lesson ends with a christological claim that comes as good news for human beings: The God-given relationship to Jesus Christ—with the life-giving benefits of salvation brought in Jesus' life that include especially his death—is the gift of life itself.

Proper 15: The Celebration

The following translation of Psalm 111 by Reginald Knox illustrates the acrostic form mentioned in the commentary.

All my heart goes out to the Lord in praise,
before the assembly where the just are gathered.
Chant we the Lord's wondrous doings,
delight and study of all who love him.
Ever his deeds are high and glorious,
faithful he abides to all eternity.
Great deeds, that he keeps still in remembrance!
He, the Lord, is kind and merciful.
In abundance he fed those who feared him,
keeping his covenant forever.
Lordly the power he showed his people,
making the lands of the heathen their possession.
No act but shows him just and faithful;
of his decrees there is no relenting.
Perpetual time shall leave them changeless;
right and truth are their foundation.
So he has brought our race deliverance;
to all eternity stands his covenant.
Unutterable is his name and worshipful;
vain without his fear is learning.
Wise evermore are you who follow it;
yours the prize that lasts for ever.
(The Holy Bible [London: Burns and Oates, 1961])

The theme of wisdom is emphasized throughout today's lessons: Solomon seeks wisdom, Christians are called to wise living, and, by extension, such living is possible only to those who abide in Christ through participation in his body and blood. The preacher may wish to examine the relationship between wisdom and mystery in the Christian experience, since in the popular mind wisdom is seen as the means of clearing up mystery rather than participating in it. Some background reading in Zen philosophy can help provide an interesting cross-cultural and theological dialogue.

The epistle lesson's emphasis on "psalms, hymns, and spiritual songs" suggests an intentional use of singing today. Summer can be a time for enjoying the "old favorites" without turning the service into a sentimental sing along. Hymns in prayer form may be used to conclude the prayer time of the congregation. Selected stanzas may be used as responses to particular acts of worship. Or, following the Pentecostal style, the opening part of the service could be a "Praise Time" where several favorite hymns might be sung. The worship leader should be responsible for such commentary as will present the hymns as preparation for and enabling of worship. In connection with the theme of wisdom, the Apostles' Creed might be used today with one or two stanzas of appropriate hymns sung in relation to each major phrase of the Creed.

Proper Sixteen
Sunday Between
August 21 and 27 Inclusive

Old Testament Texts

First Kings 8 records Solomon's dedication of the Temple. Psalm 84 celebrates worship in it.

The Lesson: *I Kings 8:(1, 6, 10-11) 22-30, 41-43*

God in the Temple

Setting. The Old Testament lesson for this Sunday brings us full cycle from where this volume began. Interpretation of Isaiah's call (Isaiah 6) for Trinity Sunday required that we explore the theological significance of the Jerusalem Temple. First Kings 8 covers the same topic but it takes us further back in time, since the text is a report of the dedication of the Jerusalem Temple. First Kings 8 suggests a lengthy history of tradition before it reached its present form. Note, for example, how Solomon is the subject of the action at the outset of v. 1 ("Then Solomon assembled the elders of Israel"), and then strangely he reenters as the object of a preposition later in the verse ("before King Solomon in Jerusalem"). This syntactical sign of editing is insignificant, but it alerts us to the possibility of several voices in the construction of the chapter, which in its present form is no less than 66 verses.

The reason for the continual expansion of this chapter is the central place of the Temple in the worship life of Israel, and the difficulty of describing how God is present with the people of God.

Structure. The focus changes somewhat as I Kings 8 develops. It begins with the report of the procession and installation of the Ark (vv. 1-13) and then shifts with the prayers of Solomon to refer more generally to the Temple (vv. 14-53) before concluding with a blessing (vv. 54-61) and an account of sacrifice (vv. 62-66).

The lectionary reading suggests vv. 1, 6, 10-11, which includes aspects of the procession and installation of the Ark. There are five stages to this liturgy: the coming together of Israel (vv. 1-3), processing with the Ark (vv. 4-5), the placing of it in the Temple (vv. 6-9), an epiphany of divine glory (vv. 10-11), and Solomon's recital of a poem or liturgy describing God's enthronement in the Temple (vv. 12-13). The suggested lectionary reading emphasizes the placing of the ark in the Temple (v. 6) and the epiphany, which signals God's presence there (vv. 10-11).

The central text is vv. 22-30, 41-43, which includes aspects of Solomon's prayer. There are four sections to this prayer: (1) petition for God to maintain the Davidic promise (vv. 23-26), (2) petition for God to hear Israel at times of distress and to forgive (vv. 27-30), (3) petition for divine help in seven different circumstances (vv. 31-32, breaking of oaths; vv. 33-34, defeat; vv. 35-36, drought; vv. 37-40, famine and plagues; vv. 41-43, foreigners; vv. 44-45, battle; and vv. 46-51 captivity), and (4) a concluding petition for God to hear (vv. 52-53). This overview of the entire prayer illustrates how the lectionary text includes the first two prayers of Solomon (vv. 23-26, and 27-30) and the fifth petition of the third prayer, which focuses on the foreigner (vv. 41-43).

Significance. There is some tension in the formation of I Kings 8 about two questions that concern divine presence: Where is God? And who is God with? The first part of the chapter is very concrete in answering these questions. God is in the Temple because that is where the Ark of the covenant is placed, and, because of this, God is with Israel. Several aspects of the procession and installation of the Ark underscore this point. The first is the concrete location of the liturgy. The Ark is being brought in specifically to the Jerusalem Temple. This is the location where God dwells in a special way. Second, the epiphany in vv. 10-11 also emphasizes how God is present in a special way. The imagery of the cloud and the glory of God are technical ways of making this point. These verses are a near repetition of the description of the tabernacle in Exodus 40:34-35, which was also covered by a cloud and so filled with the glory of God that Moses could not enter after it was first constructed. Third, the language of the old poem or cultic liturgy that Solomon recites in vv. 12-13 also underscores God's concrete presence in the Temple. This presence is particularly evident with the use of "to dwell" (Hebrew, *yašab*), which tends to signify a strong theology of divine presence or immanence in worship. An analogy to such strong language of divine presence in Christian tradition would be Communion or the Eucharist especially in traditions that confess the real presence of the risen Christ in the sacrament. These Christian traditions would also state that Christ dwells (Hebrew, *yašab*) in the bread and wine. All of these concrete images of the divine are associated with the Ark. The prayer of Solomon in the second part of the chapter turns the focus from the Ark to the Temple in general, and, with this change of focus, the imagery of God's presence also becomes less concrete. The opening line of the first prayer (vv. 23-26) expands the focus from the Temple to heaven and earth in order to describe the majesty of God. Then, the opening line of the second prayer (vv. 27-30) takes on an even more polemical tone by raising the question of whether any Temple could contain God. Finally, the reference to the foreigners in vv. 41-43 makes it clear that no one people has a corner on God.

In preaching this text it is important to underscore how I Kings 8 moves in two directions that in the end cannot be resolved in answering the questions: Where is God? And who is God with? The Ark procession states clearly that God is in worship in a concrete and special way. Thus God is with the people of God, who are gathered for worship. The prayer of Solomon builds on this confession by requesting that God hear and channel forgiveness through the Temple. But the prayer also criticizes a too exclusive and limited understanding of God. Church is not a country club, and the God who is present in worship cannot be limited to it. Thus God is potentially present to all people in all places, and those in worship who know this fact have a responsibility to communicate it rather than horde it for themselves.

The Response: *Psalm 84*

A Song of Zion

Setting. Psalm 84 consists primarily of praise in hymnic form, the central focus of which is Zion. The imagery of the psalm suggests that it was used by pilgrims who entered Jerusalem on festival occasions. Some scholars have suggested that it is liturgy used at the Temple gate.

Structure. The psalm is somewhat difficult to structure. There is a clear break between vv. 7 and 8 and then again between vv. 9 and 10. Verses 4 and 5 each begin with the same phrase, "Happy are those," which suggests that they should be grouped together. These indicators suggest a four-part division: vv. 1-3, the longing of the pilgrim for the Temple; vv. 4-7 the happiness of those who enter the Temple; vv. 8-9 a prayer for the king; and vv. 10-12 further reflections are the goodness of being in the presence of God within the Temple.

Significance. The psalm provides language that could very well accompany the narrative events of the procession of the Ark in I Kings 8. The central content of the hymn is a

171

celebration of worship that can be summarized in the three-part repetition of *happiness* in vv. 4, 5, 12. Those who are described as being happy are worshipers, and they are characterized in three ways: they live in the Temple (v. 4), they receive their strength from God (v. 5), and, finally, they trust God (v. 12).

New Testament Texts

The texts bring to a conclusion the past several weeks of readings from Ephesians and John 6. Indeed the lesson from Ephesians is the final section of practical instruction, and the verses from John come from the last several sections of Jesus' "bread of life discourse."

The Epistle: *Ephesians 6:10-20*

Dressing for God's Holy War

Setting. The author signals the beginning of the last unit of parenetic materials in v. 10, "Finally . . . ". The remarks continue through v. 20 and serve as a concluding statement to the entire practical portion of the letter (chapters 4–6). This passage is followed by only the lines of personal information (vv. 21-22) and the final benediction (vv. 23-24).

Structure. This summarizing and epitomizing section seems to have two parts, vv. 10-17 and 18-20. The first part describes Christian existence using the metaphor of putting on the spiritual armor supplied by God to believers. Then, vv. 18-20 issue a final piece of advice, calling the believers to a spiritual life of prayer that includes especially prayer for the apostle.

Significance. Recently several denominations have issued new versions of their official hymnals. Every hymnal revision committee struggled with which old hymns to delete or to include and with which new hymns to introduce. One time-worn or time-honored hymn (depending on your perspective) that had an especially hard time holding its place in new hymnals was "Onward Christian Soldiers." At least one mainline denominational hymnal did not retain this song. What was the problem? Many people considered "Onward Christian Soldiers" too militaristic. And, if we took a vote on the verses of our lesson for this week, there would be many who would advocate deleting this part of this text (vv. 10-17) from the New Testament.

Is our lesson "militaristic"? Yes and no. The passage does take up the metaphor of armor, and it does advocate that believers put on the armor of God. But look closely at the passage. The author makes clear that the struggle in which believers are engaged is real and it is dangerous. For this kind of threat the author promotes wearing God's armor. Thus we read about the enemy, the devil, and the equipment to be used against him. The text is a metaphor, a vivid one, and it may shock some to find the New Testament using such potent, if dated, military images. But, if we are honest, reading this passage is not apt to turn anyone into Christian Rambo.

There is a clear metaphorical cast to the text. The images are vivid. The author has a sense of urgency. But the text states plainly that "our struggle is not against enemies of blood and flesh." There is no call to actual martial activity, but a call to rigorous spiritual preparation for perilous spiritual conflict. Moreover, consider the list of the armor. Every piece named is overtly spiritualized: the belt of truth, the breastplate of righteousness, shoes that will make you ready to proclaim the gospel, the shield of faith, the helmet of salvation, and the sword of the Spirit. At least five of the six named items of armor are clearly defensive, not offensive. The only offensive weapon is the sword of the Spirit which is not only spiritualized (literally!) but, then, also explained as being "the word of God." Despite the correct equation of "the sword of the Spirit" with "the word of God" and the subsequent mistaken identification of "the word of God" as the Bible, there is no concrete offensive weapon in the godly Christian armor of this text. Every item is God's, and the vast majority are purely for covering and protection.

173

We have problems with passages like this one for two reasons. First, we do not take evil and its threat nearly as seriously as did the early Christians. Evil is now reduced to the sum total of human misdeeds, really nothing more or less. If we suit up against evil in our world, even for protection alone, we think primarily—if not exclusively—of human opponents. Yet, the author and those to whom he writes are not thinking in such small terms. Evil is more than human. Evil is even more than the terrible quality of heinous humanly constructed systems that come to perpetuate themselves and victimize all, even the heirs of those who created such systems. Think of apartheid. But no human made poison ivy. A world full of sinful people does not ultimately explain earthquakes, hurricanes, tidal waves, and volcanoes; and filling our world with purely lovely people will not make these shows of the forces of evil go away. The early Church knew this, and they turned to God as the source of their security and protection. They even fully relied on the message of the gospel ("the word of God") as their one weapon in the conflict they experienced with evil. Second, God is ultimately the warrior in this battle. Just as evil is small for us, so is God. Generally we consider ourselves the real doers in God's work. But the call of this text to Christians is to suit up by the grace and power of God for the purpose of steadfastness. God wages spiritual war, and by God we are protected.

Finally consider the words of the call to prayer in vv. 18-20. They speak widely, but among other things, in context, they underscore the senselessness of describing a text such as the first part of this lesson as militaristic. In our quick reactions we can misperceive and so fail to comprehend the deeper lessons of this lesson.

The Gospel: *John 6:56-69*

Faith and Awareness in Relation to Jesus Christ

Setting. We continue to read John 6 by repeating the last three verses from last Sunday's lesson and, then, moving on to consider another confrontation between Jesus and his hearers—now, remarkably, his disciples! Jesus continues to speak. We learn of his insight into his disciples and of the offense some took at him. We move finally to hear the bold confession of Simon Peter. Peter's statement is strikingly similar to his words in the Synoptic Gospels when he makes his confession at Caesarea Philippi (see Mark 8:27-30; Matthew 16:13-23; Luke 9:18-22).

Structure. Much occurs in the few verses of this lesson. Jesus speaks. His own disciples are offended, and he confronts them, so that many of them turn back from following him. Then, Jesus challenges the twelve; but Simon Peter speaks for the group, both declaring and confessing his and their convictions about Jesus. The lesson has dynamic continuity with the previous readings from John 6 in the recurrence of declaration, offense, and confrontation; but we find new elements with the introduction of challenge and confession. In addition there are important subthemes here—for example, Jesus' heavenly origins as Son of Man, flesh versus Spirit, Jesus' extraordinary knowledge, and coming to Jesus as a gift from the Father. Sorting out the moods, movements, themes, and subthemes of this passage will help develop points of view for proclamation.

Significance. One sense of the bread of life discourse left undeveloped over the past weeks is the importance of the Incarnation for understanding Jesus as the bread of life. John, like Paul and other early Christian thinkers, thought and taught about the salvific character of Jesus' death; but in relation to the images and thought patterns of the bread of life discourse, the idea of Jesus as the incarnate divine word is also crucial. Jesus is able to give life, as the bread of life, because he is the very living Word of God. In himself, not only in his death, the power of God is at work in the world granting life to the lifeless. Indeed, perhaps more than the allusions to his death, Jesus' claims about himself in this discourse are the causes for the offense taken by his hearers.

175

Jesus' statements are so startling that even his disciples are disturbed by them. Some turn away because of his claims. From the earliest days of Christian discipleship, the christological claim that Jesus is the incarnate Word, the incarnate heavenly Son, has been impossible for some to accept. Yet notice that they leave, Jesus does not send them away. He does not behave complacently in the face of their complaints, rather he bluntly acknowledges their disbelief and even explains it. His explanation may be as much or more disturbing than were the declarations about his identity and destiny. He says they do not believe because only those brought to Jesus by God can believe. In other words, even though they are disciples, their failure to believe is the conclusive proof that their discipleship was their own work and not the work of God. Belief itself is the definitive evidence of the involvement of God in the making of disciples of Jesus Christ. What about those who do not believe? What about those who once believed but now no longer can? The text has no answers. Though, notice, they left; Jesus did not drive them away. Indeed, apparently even before this confrontation, Jesus knew they did not believe in him, and he allowed them to continue to follow him as disciples.

When challenged, however, Simon Peter and the others for whom he speaks are able to articulate their faith. We hear three things: (1) Jesus is more than just another religious leader among many. Apart from him there is no other to whom believers may turn. (2) Jesus is the source of the power of life. The life he imparts is the life of God, which transforms the present and endures beyond the frail parameters of this world, because it is God's own life. And, (3) through their relationship to Jesus Christ true disciples believe and know the true identity of Jesus. This means they have faith that is more than mere facts and mere feelings, for a crucial portion of faith comes from beyond the self through the dynamics of a living relationship to Jesus Christ. There is an element of trust in this kind of faith and an awareness that brings genuine certitude for life as disciples.

Proper 16: The Celebration

The commentary on today's epistle lesson refers to the issues raised by "Onward, Christians Soldiers" as appropriate imagery for Christian hymnody. Another illustration could have been Charles Wesley's hymn based on the lesson, "Soldiers of Christ, Arise." United Methodists have tended to retain it. It has been lost in some other denominations, although it is interesting to note that it does appear in the hymnal of those pacifist folk, the Mennonites! The hymn was originally sixteen stanzas, twelve of which appeared in John Wesley's 1780 edition of *A Collection of Hymns for the Use of The People Called Methodists*. Generally, hymnals have printed only three of those at most. Following is an expanded set of stanzas which may be used selectively in the service (tune: Diademata) or which may serve as a devotional meditation upon the lesson.

> Soldiers of Christ, arise,
>   And put your armor on,
> Strong in the strength which God supplies
>   Through his eternal Son;
>   Strong in the Lord of hosts,
>   And in his mighty power,
> Who in the strength of Jesus trusts
>   Is more than conqueror.
>
> Stand then in his great might,
>   With all his strength endued,
> But take, to arm you for the fight,
>   The panoply of God;
>   That having all things done,
>   And all your conflict passed,
> Ye may o'ercome through Christ alone,
>   And stand entire at last.
>
> Stand then against your foes
>   In close and firm array;
> Legions of wily fiends oppose

177

Throughout the evil day;
But meet the sons of night,
But mock their vain design,
Armed in the arms of heavenly light,
Of righteousness divine.

Leave no unguarded place,
No weakness of the soul;
Take every virtue, every grace,
And fortify the whole;
Indissolubly joined,
To battle all proceed,
But arm yourself with all the mind
That was in Christ your head.

But above all, lay hold
On faith's victorious shield;
Armed with that adamant and gold
Be sure to win the field;
If faith surround your heart,
Satan shall be subdued,
Repelled his every fiery dart,
And quenched with Jesus' blood.

Pray, without ceasing pray
(Your Captain gives the word),
His summons cheerfully obey,
And call upon the Lord;
To God your every want
In instant prayer display;
Pray always; pray, and never faint;
Pray, without ceasing pray.

In fellowship, alone,
To God with faith draw near;
Approach his courts, beseige his throne
With all the powers of prayer.
Go to his temple, go,
Nor from his altar move;
Let every house his worship know,
And every heart his love.

Pour out your souls to God,
And bow them with your knees,
And spread your hearts and hands abroad,
And pray for Zion's peace;
Your guides and brethen bear
Forever on your mind;
Extend the arms of mighty prayer,
Ingrasping all mankind.

From strength to strength go on,
Wrestle, and fight, and pray;
Tread all the powers of darkness down,
And win the well-fought day;
Still let the Spirit cry
In all his soldiers, "Come!"
Till Christ the Lord descends from high,
And takes the conquerors home.

Stanza 7 may be used as an introit or call to worship, and stanza 8 as a call to prayer. Stanzas 1 and 2 may be used in turn before and after the reading of the Gospel, and stanza 9 could accompany the dismissal and blessing. The word *panoply* in the second stanza is a transliteration of the Greek word for "whole armor" (*panoplian*).

Scripture Index

Old Testament

A Comparison of Major Lectionaries

YEAR B: TIME AFTER PENTECOST
TRINITY SUNDAY AND PROPERS 4-16

	Old Testament	Psalm	Epistle	Gospel
		TRINITY SUNDAY		
RCL	Isa. 6:1-8	29	Rom. 8:12-17	John 3:1-17
RoCath	Deut. 4:32-34, 39-40	33:4-6, 9, 18-20, 22	Rom. 8:14-17	Matt. 28:16-20
Episcopal	Exod. 3:1-6	93		John 3:1-16
Lutheran	Deut. 6:4-9	149	Rom. 8:14-17	

PROPER 4 (May 29-June 4)
[RC: 9th Ordinary Time]
[Luth: 2nd after Pentecost]

	Old Testament	Psalm	Epistle	Gospel
RCL	I Sam. 3:1-10 (11-20)	139:1-6, 13-18	II Cor. 4:5-12	Mark 2:23-3:6
RoCath	Deut. 5:12-15	81:3-8, 10-11	II Cor. 4:6-11	
Episcopal	Deut. 5:6-21	81		Mark 2:23-28
Lutheran	Deut. 5:12-15	81:1-10		Mark 2:23-28

	Old Testament	Psalm	Epistle	Gospel
		PROPER 5 (June 5-11) [RC: 10th Ordinary Time] [Luth: 3rd after Pentecost]		
RCL	I Sam. 8:4-11 (12-15), 16-20, (11:14-15)	138	II Cor. 4:13–5:1	Mark 3:20-35
RoCath	Gen. 3:9-15	130		
Episcopal	Gen. 3:1-21	130	II Cor. 4:13-18	
Lutheran	Gen. 3:9-15	61:1-5, 8	II Cor. 4:13-18	
		PROPER 6 (June 12-18) [RC: 11th Ordinary Time] [Luth: 4th after Pentecost]		
RCL	I Sam. 15:34–16:13	20	II Cor. 5:5-10 (11-13) 14-17	Mark 4:26-34
RoCath	Ezek. 17:22-24	92:2-3, 13-16	II Cor. 5:5-10	
Episcopal	Ezek. 31:1-6, 10-14	92	II Cor. 5:1-10	
Lutheran	Ezek. 17:22-24	92:1-5 (6-10), 11-14	II Cor. 5:1-10	

	Old Testament	Psalm	Epistle	Gospel
	PROPER 7 (June 19–25) [RC: 12th Ordinary Time] [Luth: 5th after Pentecost]			
RCL	I Sam. 17: (1a, 4-11, 19-23) 32-49	9:9-20	II Cor. 6:1-13	Mark 4:35-41
RoCath	Job 38:1, 8-11	107:23-26, 28-31	II Cor. 5:14-17	
Episcopal	Job 38:1-11, 16-18	107:1-32	II Cor. 5:14-21	
Lutheran	Job 38:1-11	107:1-3, 23-32	II Cor. 5:14-21	
	PROPER 8 (June 26-July 2) [RC: 13th Ordinary Time] [Luth: 6th after Pentecost]			
RCL	II Sam. 1:1, 17-27	130	II Cor. 8:7-15	Mark 5:21-43
RoCath	Wisdom 1:13-15; 2:23-24	30:2, 4-6, 11-13	II Cor. 8:7, 9, 13-15	
Episcopal	Deut. 15:7-11	112	II Cor. 8:1-9, 13-15	Mark 5:22-24, 35b-43
Lutheran	Lam. 3:22-33	30	II Cor. 8:1-9, 13-14	Mark 5:21-24a, 35-43

185

	Old Testament	Psalm	Epistle	Gospel
PROPER 9 (July 3-9)				
[RC: 14th Ordinary Time]				
[Luth: 7th after Pentecost]				
RCL	II Sam. 5:1-5, 9-10	48	II Cor. 12:2-10	Mark 6:1-13
RoCath	Ezek. 2:2-5	123:1-4	II Cor. 12:7-10	Mark 6:1-6
Episcopal	Ezek. 2:1-7	123		Mark 6:1-6
Lutheran	Ezek. 2:1-5	143:1-2, 5-8	II Cor. 12:7-10	Mark 6:1-6
PROPER 10 (July 10-16)				
[RC: 15th Ordinary Time]				
[Luth: 8th after Pentecost]				
RCL	II Sam. 6:1-5, 12b-19	24	Eph. 1:3-14	Mark 6:14-29
RoCath	Amos 7:12-15	85:9-14	Eph. 1:1-14	Mark 6:7-13
Episcopal	Amos 7:7-15	85		Mark 6:7-13
Lutheran	Amos 7:10-15	85:8-13		Mark 6:7-13

	Old Testament	Psalm	Epistle	Gospel
PROPER 11 (July 17-23)				
[RC: 16th Ordinary Time]				
[Luth: 9th after Pentecost]				
RCL	II Sam. 7:1-14a	89:20-37	Eph. 2:11-22	Mark 6:30-34, 53-56
RoCath	Jer. 23:1-6	23	Eph. 2:13-18	Mark 6:30-34
Episcopal	Isa. 57:14b-21	22:22-30	Eph. 2:13-18	Mark 6:30-44
Lutheran	Jer. 23:1-6	23	Eph. 2:13-22	Mark 6:30-34
PROPER 12 (July 24-30)				
[RC: 17th Ordinary Time]				
[Luth: 10th after Pentecost]				
RCL	II Sam. 11:1-15	14	Eph. 3:14-21	John 6:1-21
RoCath	II Kings 4:42-44	145:10-11, 15-18	Eph. 4:1-6	John 6:1-15
Episcopal	II Kings 2:1-15	114	Eph. 4:1-7, 11-16	Mark 6:45-52
Lutheran	Exod. 24:3-11	145	Eph. 4:1-7, 11-16	John 6:1-15

	Old Testament	Psalm	Epistle	Gospel
	PROPER 13 (July 31–Aug. 6)			
	[RC. 18th Ordinary Time]			
	[Luth: 11th after Pentecost]			
RCL	II Sam. 11:26–12:13a	51:1-12	Eph. 4:1-16	John 6:24-35
RoCath	Exod. 16:2-4, 12-15	78:3-4, 23-25, 54	Eph. 4:17, 20-24	
Episcopal	Exod. 16:2-4, 9-15	78:1-25	Eph. 4:17-25	
Lutheran	Exod. 16:2-15	78:23-29	Eph. 4:17-24	
	PROPER 14 (Aug. 7-13)			
	[RC: 19th Ordinary Time]			
	[Luth: 12th after Pentecost]			
RCL	II Sam. 18:5-9, 15, 31-33	130	Eph. 4:25–5:2	John 6:35, 41-51
RoCath	I Kings 19:4-8	34:2-9	Eph. 4:30–5:2	John 6:41-51
Episcopal	Deut. 8:1-10	34		John 6:37-51
Lutheran	I Kings 19:4-8	34:1-8	Eph. 4:30–5:2	John 6:41-51

	Old Testament	Psalm	Epistle	Gospel
PROPER 15 (Aug. 14-20) [RC: 20th Ordinary Time] [Luth: 13th after Pentecost]				
RCL	I Kings 2:10-12; 3:3-14	111	Eph. 5:15-20	John 6:51-58
RoCath	Prov. 9:1-6	34:2-3, 10-15		
Episcopal	Prov. 9:1-6	147		John 6:53-59
Lutheran	Prov. 9:1-6	34:9-14		
PROPER 16 (Aug. 21-27) [RC: 21st Ordinary Time] [Luth: 14th after Pentecost]				
RCL	I Kings 3:(1, 6, 10-11) 22-30, 41-43	84	Eph. 6:10-20	John 6:56-69
RoCath	Joshua 24:1-2, 15-18	34:2-3, 16-23	Eph. 5:21-32	John 6:60-69
Episcopal	Joshua 24:1-2a, 15-25	16	Eph. 5:21-33	John 6:60-69
Lutheran	Joshua 24:1-2a, 14-18	34:15-22	Eph. 5:21-31	John 6:60-69

A Liturgical Calendar

Trinity Sunday Through August 1997–2006

	1998 B	1999 C	2000 A	2001 B	2002 C
Trinity	June 7	May 30	June 18	June 10	May 26
Proper 4	——	——	——	——	June 2
Proper 5	——	June 6	——	——	June 9
Proper 6	June 14	June 13	——	June 17	June 16
Proper 7	June 21	June 20	June 25	June 24	June 23
Proper 8	June 28	June 27	July 2	July 1	June 30
Proper 9	July 5	July 4	July 9	July 8	July 7
Proper 10	July 12	July 11	July 16	July 15	July 14
Proper 11	July 19	July 18	July 23	July 22	July 21
Proper 12	July 26	July 25	July 30	July 29	July 28
Proper 13	Aug. 2	Aug. 1	Aug. 6	Aug. 5	Aug. 4
Proper 14	Aug. 9	Aug. 8	Aug. 13	Aug. 12	Aug. 11
Proper 15	Aug. 16	Aug. 15	Aug. 20	Aug. 19	Aug. 18
Proper 16	Aug. 23	Aug. 22	Aug. 27	Aug. 26	Aug. 25
Proper 17	Aug. 30	Aug. 29	Sept. 3	Sept. 2	——

	2003 B	2004 C	2005 A	2006 B	2007 C
Trinity	June 15	June 6	May 22	June 11	May 27
Proper 4	———	———	May 29	———	June 3
Proper 5	———	———	June 5	———	June 10
Proper 6	———	June 13	June 12	June 18	June 17
Proper 7	June 22	June 20	June 19	June 25	June 24
Proper 8	June 29	June 27	June 26	July 2	July 1
Proper 9	July 6	July 4	July 3	July 9	July 8
Proper 10	July 13	July 11	July 10	July 16	July 15
Proper 11	July 20	July 18	July 17	July 23	July 22
Proper 12	July 27	July 25	July 24	July 30	July 29
Proper 13	Aug. 3	Aug. 1	July 31	Aug. 6	Aug. 5
Proper 14	Aug. 10	Aug. 8	Aug. 7	Aug. 13	Aug. 12
Proper 15	Aug. 17	Aug. 15	Aug. 14	Aug. 20	Aug. 19
Proper 16	Aug. 24	Aug. 22	Aug. 21	Aug. 27	Aug. 26
Proper 17	Aug. 31	Aug. 29	Aug. 28	———	———